P9-CIW-131

THE Cloud Collector's HANDBOOK

This cloud collection belongs to:

....

THE
Cloud Collector's
HANDBOOK

BY *Gavin Pretor-Pinney*

❖

An official publication of
THE CLOUD APPRECIATION SOCIETY
www.cloudappreciationsociety.org

Image research by society photo editor, Ian Loxley (Member 1868).
Meteorological guidance by Stephen Burt (Member 2814)
of the Royal Meteorological Society.

CHRONICLE BOOKS
SAN FRANCISCO

First published in the United States in 2011 by Chronicle Books.

First published in the United Kingdom in 2009 by Sceptre, an imprint
of Hodder & Stoughton, an Hachette UK company.

Copyright © 2011 by Gavin Pretor-Pinney.
Copyright of the individual photographs remains with the credited
photographers.

Library of Congress Cataloging-in-Publication Data is available.

ISBN: 978-0-8118-7542-4

Manufactured in China

Designed by Suzanne LaGasa

10 9 8 7 6 5 4

Chronicle Books LLC
680 Second Street
San Francisco, California 94107
www.chroniclebooks.com

Contents & Scorecard

Enter your totals in pencil, and copy them onto page 9 for a running tally of your score.

How to Collect Clouds

You might well think that cloud collecting sounds like a ridiculous idea. How can anyone collect such ephemeral and free-spirited things as clouds? Surely, they're just about as uncollectable as anything gets.

Magicked into being by the inscrutable laws of the atmosphere, clouds exist in a constant state of flux, shifting effortlessly from one form to another. One moment, they're joining and spreading into undulating layers. The next, they're breaking into torn shreds. One moment, they're building upward in enormous, weighty towers with dark, brooding bases. The next, they're cascading back down in delicate, translucent streaks. And then they're gone—shedding their moisture as rain or just evaporating into the blue. They're like expressions on the face of the sky, and certainly not candidates for a display case. Given all the possible things you might consider collecting, clouds would seem to be a completely silly option.

But that's where you'd be wrong. You don't have to own something to collect it. You don't even have to hold it. You just have to notice it and record it.

And that is what this handbook is for. The entries will help you identify a whole range of distinctive cloud types, and some of the amazing optical effects produced by clouds as they scatter the sunlight. When you spot a particular cloud type, add it to your collection by noting down the details on the relevant page. Ideally, keep a camera at hand so that you can back up your claims with photographic evidence.

With each addition to your collection, you earn cloud-collecting points, which are determined by how hard each cloud or effect is to see. While a common old Stratocumulus cloud only earns you 10 points, the fleeting crescent of a horseshoe vortex earns 50 points. The maximum score of 55 belongs to the rare and dramatic breaking waves of the Kelvin-Helmholtz cloud—the jewel of any cloud collection.

Altocumulus lenticularis, ruddy from another long day of being a beautiful cloud.

Your points should be entered religiously on the Contents & Scorecard on page 5 and, as they mount up, they should be counted and re-counted with a greedy cackle. They'll be essential in judging the worth of your collection, and fueling the bitter rivalry that will develop with fellow cloudspotters.

This handbook is intended to work as a complement to your own photographic records. Of course, you don't have to take pictures, but few cloudspotters can resist. All the photographs here were taken by members of the Cloud Appreciation Society, and can be seen much larger on the society's Web site, along with tips on cloud photography (see Web address on page 8). As the physical manifestation of your cloud collection, such photographic records of meteorological moments serve as something to rifle through and caress back at home.

The system for naming clouds is rather like that for plants and animals, and uses Latin terms to divide them up into different genera, species and varieties. Only the more distinctive and recognizable cloud types are included here. An overview of all the officially recognized classifications appears on pages 136-137. Technical terms used in the cloud explanations are written in italics and explained on pages 132-135. Remember, cloudscapes usually contain a whole range of different cloud types, so don't expect them always to have the orderly, distinct forms of these images.

While it may not have the permanence of a collection of coins, nor the swapability of one of rare stamps, there's something honest about a collection of clouds. Clouds embody the impermanence of the world around us. "Nature," wrote Ralph Waldo Emerson, "is a mutable cloud which is always and never the same."

Gavin Pretor-Pinney,

The Cloud Appreciation Society
www.cloudappreciationsociety.org/collecting

How Much Is Your Collection Worth?

As you add clouds to your collection, update the totals in pencil from the scorecard on page 5.

Total A		max: 350
Total B		max: 350
Total C		max: 350
Total D		max: 525
Total E		max: 425
Cloud-Collecting Grand Total:		Maximum score is 2,000

Cumulus

Left: A Cumulus congestus tower. *Right:* Cumulus fractus (as it forms/evaporates).

If you've never spotted a Cumulus cloud, then you ought to get out more. This has to be one of the easiest types to add to your cloud collection (which explains why it earns a low score). Cumulus clouds are the cotton-wool puffs, with flat bases, that drift lazily across the sky on a sunny day. Generally forming a few hours after daybreak, they tend to dissipate before sundown, for they form on thermals—invisible columns of air rising from the ground as it is warmed by the Sun.

Most forms of Cumulus produce no rain or snow, and so are known as fair-weather clouds. But in *unstable air,* their bright, crisp cauliflower mounds can build upwards so that they develop from the small humilis *species* through mediocris to the largest form, Cumulus congestus. With its ominous, shadowy base, this cloud is no longer fair-weather. Congestus can produce brief but sizeable showers, and can keep growing into fierce Cumulonimbus storm clouds (page 30).

The little ones, by contrast, are only scary when they take the form of David Hasselhoff.

CUMULUS SPECIES:
- **Humilis:** wider than it is tall.
- **Mediocris:** as tall as it is wide.
- **Congestus:** taller than it is wide.
- **Fractus:** broken, with ragged edges.

CUMULUS VARIETIES:
- **Radiatus:** lined up in "cloud streets" (p. 46).

Known as fair-weather clouds, Cumulus tend to appear on sunny days.

CLOUD-COLLECTING POINTS

○ 15 points: Any Cumulus

○ 15 points: Bonus for collecting all four species (see opposite): humilis, mediocris, congestus, fractus

+ Add Total To Page 5

Typical altitudes: 1,000–5,000 ft.

Precipitation: none, except for brief showers from Cumulus congestus.

Don't confuse with: Stratocumulus (p. 12), Altocumulus (p. 18), Cumulonimbus (p. 30).

○ *I spotted Cumulus*

DATE   TIME

LOCATION

WEATHER CONDITIONS

IMAGE FILE NAME(S)

Stratocumulus

When Cumulus clouds become so plentiful that they join together and cover the sky, they are known as Stratocumulus.

The most widespread of all cloud types, Stratocumulus is a low layer or patch of cloud that has a well-defined, clumpy base. The patches are either joined up or have gaps in between. When the sky is overcast, and the cloud base appears to be low, with tones from white to dark grey, cloudspotters can confidently add Stratocumulus to their cloud collections.

High Stratocumulus that have *cloudlets* with gaps in between—a variety known as perlucidus—can be confused with the midlevel cloud Altocumulus (page 18). But Stratocumulus is usually less orderly in appearance and its cloudlets are bigger (appearing larger than the width of three fingers, held at arm's length, when they are more than 30 degrees above the horizon).

Due to its sun-blocking tendencies, Stratocumulus may not be the most popular cloud, but it is one of the most varied.

STRATOCUMULUS SPECIES:

○ **Stratiformis:** extends over large areas of sky, rather than forming in patches.

○ **Lenticularis:** smooth, lens-shaped mass (p. 34).

○ **Castellanus:** top of the layer rises in turrets (p. 40).

STRATOCUMULUS VARIETIES:

○ **Translucidus:** thin enough to show the outline of the Sun or Moon.

○ **Perlucidus:** gaps between clumps.

○ **Opacus:** thick enough to mask the Sun or Moon completely.

○ **Duplicatus:** more than one layer, sometimes partly merged (p. 48).

○ **Undulatus:** wave-like (p. 42).

○ **Radiatus:** lined-up clumps that converge towards horizon (p. 46).

○ **Lacunosus:** layer contains large holes, fringed with cloud (p. 44).

On a flight from Hanoi to Kuala Lumpur, by Ruziana Mohd Mokhtar (Member 14191)

Above: The ever-varied and omnipresent tones of Stratocumulus clouds.
Next page: A high Stratocumulus.

CLOUD-COLLECTING POINTS

○ 10 points: Any Stratocumulus

○ 10 points: Bonus for when sunlight streams down through holes in the layer, like huge torch beams (see p. 108)

+ Add Total To Page 7

Typical altitudes: 1,000–4,500 ft.

Precipitation: occasionally light rain, snow or snow pellets.

Don't confuse with: Cumulus (p. 10), Stratus (p. 16), Altocumulus (p. 18).

○ *I Spotted Stratocumulus*

DATE   TIME

LOCATION

WEATHER CONDITIONS

IMAGE FILE NAME(S)

Stratus

Stratus fractus on a mountainside.

The lowest-forming of all the cloud types, Stratus can give you a strangely claustrophobic feeling, even though you're outside. It is a featureless, grey overcast layer, which lurks around with its base generally no higher than 1,500 feet from the ground. This is much lower than its equally charisma-free cousin, the Altostratus cloud (page 20). Stratus can sometimes obscure the tops of tall buildings. When a cloud like this forms so low that it is at ground level, it is known as fog or mist. Since fog can sometimes form in a different way from airborne Stratus, it has a page of its own (page 90).

One way that Stratus forms is when moist air cools as it blows over a relatively cold surface, such as a cold sea or land covered in thawing snow ("advection fog" [see page 90] is formed in the same way when winds are gentler). Another is when air cools as it rises. This might be as it blows up the lower slopes of a mountainside or as warmer air slowly rides up over a region of colder (denser) air. Finally, Stratus can appear when fog, which has formed overnight, lifts from the ground as it is stirred by a freshening wind.

STRATUS SPECIES:

○ **Nebulosus:** a grey, featureless layer—by far the most common form.

○ **Fractus:** patches or broken wisps, e.g., on hillsides. Known as pannus (p. 54) when forms in damp air below rain clouds.

STRATUS VARIETIES:

○ **Opacus:** thick enough to mask the Sun or Moon completely.

○ **Translucidus:** thin enough to show the outline of the Sun or Moon.

○ **Undulatus:** surface of the layer has a wave-like appearance. Since the cloud layer is so diffuse, this variety is very rarely observed (p. 42).

Over Bolungarvík, Iceland, by Michèle Gruber (Member 11072).

"I'd like to cancel my booking for the penthouse restaurant, please."

CLOUD-COLLECTING POINTS

○ 15 points: Any Stratus

○ 20 points: Bonus for when you are able to look down on to Stratus and notice its undulating upper surface

+ Add Total To Page 5

Typical altitudes: 0–1,500 ft.

Precipitation: just occasional drizzle, light snow or snow grains.

Don't confuse with: Altostratus (p. 20), Cirrostratus (p. 26), Nimbostratus (p. 28).

○ *I Spotted Stratus*

DATE   TIME

LOCATION

WEATHER CONDITIONS

IMAGE FILE NAME(S)

Altocumulus

These are typically midlevel layers or patches of *cloudlets,* which form clumps or rolls. They are white or grey, and shaded on the side away from the Sun. This distinguishes Altocumulus from the shade-free cloudlets of Cirrocumulus (page 24). Another distinguishing feature is the size of its cloudlets. These appear between the width of one and three fingers, held at arm's length, when they're more than 30 degrees above the horizon.

The species of Altocumulus that stands out from all the others is lenticularis, described on page 34. Rather than a layer of cloudlets, it has the form of large, smooth individual clouds.

Top: Altocumulus undulatus. *Bottom:* Jellyfish trails, known as virga (page 58).

With no less than four possible species and seven varieties, Altocumulus clouds produce the most dramatic and beautiful cloudscapes, especially in the rays of a low Sun.

ALTOCUMULUS SPECIES:

O **Stratiformis:** extends over large areas of sky, rather than forming in patches.

O **Lenticularis:** smooth, lens-shaped mass (p. 34).

O **Castellanus:** top of the layer rises in turrets (p. 40).

O **Floccus:** Cumulus-like cloudlets, with ragged bases, often with virga (p. 60).

ALTOCUMULUS VARIETIES:

O **Translucidus:** thin enough to show the outline of the Sun or Moon.

O **Perlucidus:** gaps between clumps.

O **Opacus:** thick enough to mask the Sun or Moon completely.

O **Duplicatus:** more than one layer, sometimes partly merged (p. 48).

O **Undulatus:** wave-like (p. 42).

O **Radiatus:** lined-up clumps that converge toward horizon (p. 46).

O **Lacunosus:** layer contains large holes, fringed with cloud (p. 44).

Altocumulus: who knocked over the jar of cotton balls?

CLOUD-COLLECTING POINTS:

○ 30 points: Any Altocumulus

○ 15 points: Bonus if it's at sunrise or sunset, when this cloud is beautiful enough to rival any other

+ Add Total To Page 5

Typical altitudes: 6,500-20,000 ft.

Precipitation: none, except, very occasionally, light rain from castellanus.

Don't confuse with: Stratocumulus (p. 12), Cirrocumulus (p. 24).

○ *I spotted Altocumulus*

DATE   TIME

LOCATION

WEATHER CONDITIONS

IMAGE FILE NAME(S)

Altostratus

Streaks, known as Altostratus undulatus radiatus.

It feels wrong to devote as much space to the rather drab and featureless Altostratus cloud as to its relative, the gloriously varied Altocumulus. Few cloud-spotters will be seen to punch the air and high-five upon adding this one to their cloud collection. Altostratus is, after all, generally considered the most boring of all the cloud types. Although, even to say that, makes it sound rather more noteworthy than it deserves.

Altostratus is a midlevel, generally featureless, grey, overcast layer— a Tupperware sky that often extends over several thousand square miles. True to its dull nature, Altostratus produces little more than a lingering drizzle or light snow. Once it is thick enough to produce more significant precipitation, it has generally developed into the Nimbostratus cloud (page 28).

The most common way for Altostratus to form is by the thickening of high Cirrostratus (page 26), when a large region of warmer air pushes against one of colder air. The warmer air, being less dense, rises gently en masse over the colder.

Generally darker than Stratus (page 16), Altostratus never produces *halo phenomena*, as Cirrostratus does. When you can see the Sun, it appears as if through ground glass.

THERE ARE NO ALTOSTRATUS SPECIES.

ALTOSTRATUS VARIETIES:

○ **Translucidus:** thin enough to show the outline of the Sun or Moon.

○ **Opacus:** thick enough to mask the Sun or Moon completely.

○ **Duplicatus:** more than one layer, visible only in the glancing light of a low Sun (p. 48).

○ **Undulatus:** wave-like (p. 42).

○ **Radiatus:** rows that converge toward horizon; very occasional form (p. 46).

Extra points for managing to stay awake when you watch Altostratus.

CLOUD-COLLECTING POINTS:

○ 15 points: Any Altostratus

○ 10 points: Bonus for managing to persuade anyone else to take the slightest bit of interest in this cloud

+ Add Total To Page 5

Typical altitudes: 6,500–16,500 ft. The cloud base lowers as it thickens.

Precipitation: prolonged, but light.

Don't confuse with: Stratus (p. 16), Cirrostratus (p. 26).

○ *I Spotted Altostratus*

DATE   TIME

LOCATION

WEATHER CONDITIONS

IMAGE FILE NAME(S)

Cirrus

Top: Twisted tousles of Cirrus intortus.
Bottom: Cirrus spissatus lingers after a Cumulonimbus (page 30) has dissipated.

The most ethereal looking of all the main types, Cirrus clouds are also the highest—composed entirely of ice crystals. These typically fall through the high winds of the upper *troposphere* to appear as delicate, celestial brush strokes, known as "fallstreaks." Cirrus often look like white locks of hair (from which the Latin name is derived).

Cirrus clouds thickening and spreading across the blue can be the first signs of moisture developing at high altitudes, indicating the start of a common cloud progression that leads to Nimbostratus (page 28) and produces rain or snow in a day or so.

Apart from the thick Cirrus spissatus (see below), all other forms of Cirrus can *refract* and reflect the sunlight to produce colored arcs and rings, called *halo phenomena* (see pages 120-131).

CIRRUS SPECIES:

○ **Fibratus:** individual filaments without hooks or clumps at the end (p. 38).

○ **Uncinus:** fallstreaks are shaped like hooks or commas.

○ **Spissatus:** thick patches—sometimes as the anvil from an old Cumulonimbus (p. 30).

○ **Castellanus:** fallstreaks from tiny tufts with turreted tops (p. 40).

○ **Floccus:** fallstreaks from individual rounded tufts.

CIRRUS VARIETIES:

○ **Intortus:** irregular, tangled fallstreaks.

○ **Radiatus:** parallel filaments, usually aligned to the wind, converge toward horizon (p. 46).

○ **Vertebratus:** filaments look like a fish skeleton with a central spine.

○ **Duplicatus:** filaments or streaks in more than one layer (p. 48).

Cirrus clouds are streaks of falling ice crystals. This is the hooked species, uncinus.

CLOUD-COLLECTING POINTS:

○ 20 points: Any Cirrus

○ 15 points: Bonus for the classic uncinus species with its distinctive hooked formation (above)

+ Add Total To Page 5

Typical altitudes: 20,000-40,000 ft.

Precipitation: none reaching ground.

Don't confuse with: Altocumulus (p. 18) that is producing trails of precipitation, known as virga (p. 60).

○ *I spotted Cirrus*

DATE   TIME

LOCATION

WEATHER CONDITIONS

IMAGE FILE NAME(S)

Cirrocumulus

Cirrocumulus appears more often in patches than spread across the sky.

These are high patches or layers of *cloudlets* that appear tiny, on account of their distance from the ground.

The best way to distinguish Cirrocumulus from lower Altocumulus (page 18) is the size of the cloudlets, as well as the area of the sky covered by the layer as a whole. Being such a distance from the ground (often in the region of six miles), the cloudlets of Cirrocumulus appear so small that you often have to look carefully to notice the cloud's grainy texture. For the cloud to be Cirrocumulus, these cloudlets must appear no larger than the width of a finger, held at arm's length, when they are more than 30 degrees above the horizon.

Composed almost entirely of ice crystals, Cirrocumulus is actually a rare and fleeting cloud. Mostly, when you see a layer of cloudlets, they belong to the lower water-droplet cloud, Altocumulus. That's why Cirrocumulus is a big points earner, one of the highest scoring of the main cloud types.

CIRROCUMULUS SPECIES:

○ **Stratiformis:** extends over large areas of sky, rather than forming in patches.

○ **Lenticularis:** smooth, lens-shaped mass (p. 34).

○ **Castellanus:** tops of cloudlets have turrets (p. 40)—you'll certainly need binoculars to see this.

○ **Floccus:** Cumulus-like cloudlets, with ragged bases, often with virga (p 60).

CIRROCUMULUS VARIETIES:

○ **Undulatus:** wave-like (p. 42).

○ **Lacunosus:** layer contains large holes, fringed with cloud (p. 44).

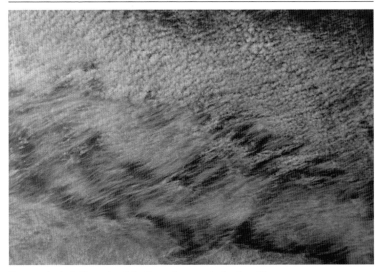

Cirrocumulus looks like grains of rice thrown for some skydiver's wedding.

CLOUD-COLLECTING POINTS:

○ 40 points: Any Cirrocumulus

○ 10 points: Bonus for when it's near Cirrus (p. 22) and patches of Cirrostratus (p. 26), since they often form together

+ Add Total To Page 5

Typical altitudes: 25,000–35,000 ft.

Precipitation: none reaching ground.

Don't confuse with: the larger cloudlets of the midlevel Altocumulus (p. 18)—a much more common cloud.

○ *I Spotted Cirrocumulus*

DATE   TIME

LOCATION

WEATHER CONDITIONS

IMAGE FILE NAME(S)

Cirrostratus

Top: A halo like this indicates a Cirrostratus cloud. **Bottom:** A milky veil.

Cirrostratus is a subtle, understated cloud that can easily go unnoticed—except, that is, by cloudspotters keen to complete their collection of the ten main cloud types.

A delicate layer of ice crystals, often spread over vast areas of the sky, Cirrostratus can appear as no more than a light, milky whitening of the blue. It can sometimes look striped or fibrous (the species known as fibratus), but more commonly lacks any variation in tone.

It also distinguishes itself as the best of the high clouds at producing *halo phenomena* (see pages 120–131). A range of arcs, rings and points of light can appear as the sunlight is *refracted* and reflected by its tiny ice crystals. These don't always appear but, when they do, can exhibit beautiful rainbow colors. The presence of haloes is a sure way to distinguish Cirrostratus from Altostratus, which, being lower and consisting (at least partially) of droplets, doesn't produce them.

CIRROSTRATUS SPECIES:

O **Fibratus:** made of delicate, parallel fibers (p. 38).

O **Nebulosus:** smooth, with no variation in tone.

CIRROSTRATUS VARIETIES:

O **Duplicatus:** more than one layer at different altitudes; very hard to distinguish unless differing winds at each altitude cause fibratus stripes to point in different directions (p. 48).

O **Undulatus:** wave-like (p. 42).

Top: over Battle, East Sussex, UK, by Graham Keen (Member 7967)

Cirrostratus consists of ice crystals and, like this one, may appear fibrous.

CLOUD-COLLECTING POINTS:

○ 20 points: Any Cirrostratus

○ 20 points: Bonus for noticing Cirrostratus producing more than one halo phenomenon (see pp. 120–131) at a time

+ Add Total To Page 5

Typical altitudes: 16,500-30,000 ft.

Precipitation: none.

Don't confuse with: lower and thicker Stratus (p. 16), Altostratus (p. 20), which don't form halo phenomena.

○ *I Spotted Cirrostratus*

DATE   TIME

LOCATION

WEATHER CONDITIONS

IMAGE FILE NAME(S)

Nimbostratus

These clouds can also produce snow.

When people claim clouds are depressing, they're often thinking of Nimbostratus. This thick, grey, featureless rain cloud gives all the other ones a bad name. Not only does it block much of the Sun's rays, casting everything in a dim, miserable light, it also produces rain—and lots of it.

Nimbostratus is one of only two cloud types that are defined as always producing rain or other precipitation. The other is the Cumulonimbus storm cloud (page 30). From below, both appear as dark and ominous skies, but they can be distinguished by the nature of their precipitation. Compared with the brief heavy showers from individual Cumulonimbus clouds, the precipitation from Nimbostratus is much more steady, and can last for many hours.

Surreptitiously and without fanfare is how the Nimbostratus arrives. It generally results from the thickening and lowering of Altostratus (page 20). Since one cloud leads to the other, the point of distinction between Alto- and Nimbostratus is rather academic. But when the cloud is dark, and the rain moderate to heavy, and its diffused base shows darker ragged patches of Stratus fractus, which is also known as pannus (page 54), you can confidently add Nimbostratus to your cloud collection.

But you're unlikely to win any awards for your photos of this less than handsome cloud.

NIMBOSTRATUS SPECIES & VARIETIES:

○ Being such a featureless wet blanket of a cloud, Nimbostratus is not considered to have any species or varieties.

Over Glossop, Derbyshire, UK, by Dave Leech (Member 12529)

A lovely day by the seaside, courtesy of the Nimbostratus cloud.

CLOUD-COLLECTING POINTS:

○ 10 points: Any Nimbostratus

○ 5 points: Bonus to make you feel better if the Nimbostratus turns your weekend at the beach into a washout

+ Add Total To Page 5

Typical altitudes: 0-10,000 ft.

Precipitation: you bet.

Don't confuse with: Stratus (p. 16), Altostratus (p. 20), Cumulonimbus (p. 30) if you are directly below it.

○ *I spotted Nimbostratus*

DATE   TIME

LOCATION

WEATHER CONDITIONS

IMAGE FILE NAME(S)

Cumulonimbus

A bad hair day for a Cumulonimbus capillatus.

No cloud collection is complete without the big one, the Godfather of clouds: Cumulonimbus. This enormous storm cloud, which is often in the shape of a blacksmith's anvil, can form individually or coordinate with neighbors to form *multicell* and *supercell storms*.

Cloudspotters should note that the anvil shape is visible only when looking at the cloud from many miles away. It develops from Cumulus congestus (page 10), and is a Cumulonimbus once its summit has changed from droplets to ice crystals—developing softer edges. Below a Cumulonimbus, you will see just its dark, ragged underside, which (being so low) appears to cover the whole sky. Distinguish it from Nimbostratus by how its moisture falls (see page 28), and the fact that it produces thunder, lightning and often hail.

Cumulonimbus also gives rise to a whole range of *accessory clouds* and *supplementary features*, such as incus (page 70), mamma (page 56), pileus (page 50), velum (page 52), arcus (page 64) and tuba (page 68).

CUMULONIMBUS SPECIES: (Only distinguishable when the cloud is many miles away.)

○ **Calvus:** top is of soft mounds, and isn't fibrous or striated (means 'bald' in Latin).

○ **Capillatus:** developing from calvus into mature phase, top spreads out into familiar anvil plume of Cirrus-like fibers or striations (means "hairy" in Latin).

THERE ARE NO CUMULONIMBUS VARIETIES.

Above: View from below.
Next page: The Cumulonimbus, King of Clouds, can sometimes grow to over ten miles high.

CLOUD-COLLECTING POINTS:

○ 40 points: Any Cumulonimbus

○ 15 points: Bonus for when the King of Clouds is producing thunder and lightning

+ Add Total To Page 5

Typical altitudes: bases around 2,000 ft, can reach up to 45,000 ft.

Precipitation: heavy showers, often hail.

Don't confuse with: Cumulus congestus (p. 10), Nimbostratus (p. 28).

○ *I Spotted Cumulonimbus*

DATE   TIME

LOCATION

WEATHER CONDITIONS

IMAGE FILE NAME(S)

Lenticularis

Lenticularis species of high Cirrus cloud.

Lenticularis clouds are contenders for the Weirdest-Looking-Clouds-in-the-Sky awards. Their name is Latin for a lentil, on account of their very distinctive disc shapes. They often look remarkably like flying saucers. Presumably, when they were named, no one could think of the Latin word for "shaped like a UFO."

Lenticularis can be found at low, medium and high *cloud levels*, although the most striking and dramatic ones tend to be the midlevel Altocumulus lenticularis. At whatever altitude they form, they are usually caused by a moist airstream flowing over raised ground, such as a hill or mountain peak. When the atmosphere in the area is *stable*, the air can develop a wave-like motion downstream, invisibly rising and dipping in the lee of the peak. If the air rises and cools enough, lenticularis clouds can appear at the crests of these waves. Unlike most clouds that drift along with the breeze, these hover even in the strongest winds (so long as air speed remains constant). Their positions in the airstream remain fixed, like the stationary waves of water behind a boulder in the current of a fast-moving stream.

When the airstream contains layers of moist air separated by drier air, a stacked formation can appear, known as "pile d'assiettes" (which is French for "your turn to do the dishes"—shown on the following two pages).

Over Watlington, Oxfordshire, UK, by Richard B. Machin (Member 10911)

Above: low Stratocumulus Lenticularis.
Next page: Altocumulus lenticularis stacked in pile d'assiettes formation.

CLOUD-COLLECTING POINTS:

○ 45 points: Any lenticularis

○ 25 points: Bonus for the rare pile d'assiettes, formed due to alternating layers of moister and drier air

+ Add Total To Page 5

Species is found in: Stratocumulus (p 12), Altocumulus (p. 18), Cirrocumulus (p. 24).

Don't confuse with: pileus (p. 50), which only differs in that it forms over Cumulus clouds, not hills.

○ *I spotted lenticularis*

DATE   TIME

LOCATION

WEATHER CONDITIONS

IMAGE FILE NAME(S)

Fibratus

The high, ice-crystal clouds of Cirrus (page 22) and Cirrostratus (page 26) are called fibratus when they have been drawn out by the wind into long, fine filaments. These close strands of cloud appear rather like hair run through with a comb. Such an orderly atmospheric hairstyle depends on high, continuous winds. These are more common up at Cirrus and Cirrostratus level, since the higher you climb through the *troposphere*, the faster the average wind speed becomes, and the less the wind is messed about by the influence of the ground.

Father Christmas's beard, or the delicate strands of Cirrostratus fibratus.

The way to distinguish fibratus from the other Cirrus species that can also have somewhat parallel filaments, floccus and uncinus (see page 22), is to look at the ends of the strands. In fibratus, the filaments do not descend from the fluffy tufts of cloud found in floccus, nor do they curve down from thicker heads to give the hooked, comma-like appearance of uncinus. Fibratus are simply thin, delicate strands of high cloud.

As expressions on the face of the sky, clouds can be indicators of the atmosphere's moods, but not so in the case of fibratus clouds. Other than indicating high, continuous winds up at cloud level, they tell nothing of the weather in store.

Perhaps they are there just to look nice.

Cirrus fibratus stretching off to the distance are also known as radiatus.

CLOUD-COLLECTING POINTS:

○ 15 points: Any fibratus

○ 10 points: Bonus for when the hair-like strands have been blown into a fashionable, wavy style

+ Add Total To Page 5

Species is found in: Cirrus (p. 22), Cirrostratus (p. 26).

Don't confuse with: uncinus and floccus species of Cirrus clouds (see opposite and p. 22).

○ *I spotted fibratus*

DATE   TIME

LOCATION

WEATHER CONDITIONS

IMAGE FILE NAME(S)

Castellanus

Aerial fortifications called castellanus.

When a layer of cloud rises in distinct turrets with bumpy tops that resemble crenellations, it is of the species known as castellanus—and this one can give an early indication of unsettled weather to come later in the day.

The turrets of castellanus can be found at all three *cloud levels*, but the ones that are hardest to identify are in the high clouds, Cirrocumulus (page 24) and Cirrus (page 22). As much as anything, this is because the cloud elements are so far away that they appear tiny from the ground, making any observation of the subtle nature of their tops rather challenging. Luckily, these examples of castellanus are also the least indicative of unsettled weather.

The low cloud, Stratocumulus (page 12), may be described as castellanus when at least some of the cauliflower mounds that form its upper surface have grown taller than they are wide. These rising turrets can sometimes continue to grow upward and develop into rain-bearing Cumulus congestus (page 10), or even Cumulonimbus (page 30) storm clouds.

But it is in the Midlevel cloud, Altocumulus (page 18), that the jagged crenellations of castellanus are most recognizable, and also where they best forecast unsettled weather. The vigorous turrets show that the air at the midcloud level is *unstable*. Any Cumulus that start to develop on thermals will, upon reaching this layer, continue growing with extra vigor and quite possibly develop into tall, stormy Cumulonimbus clouds.

Altocumulus clouds are the best ones to look at for the turreted tops of castellanus.

CLOUD-COLLECTING POINTS:

○ 25 points: Any castellanus

○ 20 points: Bonus for correctly predicting showers later in the day by spotting some at the Altocumulus level

+ Add Total To Page 5

Species is found in: Stratocumulus (p. 12), Altocumulus (p. 18), Cirrus (p. 22), Cirrocumulus (p. 24).

Don't confuse with: floccus, whose cloudlets lack pronounced turrets.

○ *I spotted castellanus*

DATE   TIME

LOCATION

WEATHER CONDITIONS

IMAGE FILE NAME(S)

Undulatus

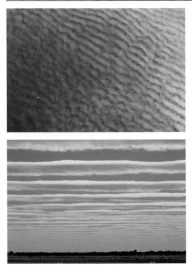

Top: Altocumulus undulatus.
Bottom: Stratocumulus undulatus.

When the surface of a cloud layer, or the arrangement of its *cloudlets*, develops an undulating appearance that suggests waves, it's defined as the undulatus variety.

Waves and clouds have always had a close relationship. The interaction of currents in the atmosphere, and the effects of the terrain on the passage of winds, can result in a whole range of undulating currents of air. Generally, these are invisible, unless the rising parts of the undulations cool the air enough to produce clouds of droplets or ice crystals, which are thinner or absent in the sinking parts of the undulations. In such circumstances, the waves show up on the surface of the cloud or as cloud billows with gaps in between.

Undulatus usually forms when the air above and below the cloud layer is moving at differing speeds and/or in different directions. It is the shearing effect of the two airstreams that gives rise to the cloud billows, which resemble ripples on a sandy beach caused by the movement of water.

Wave formations in clouds are so common that the undulatus variety is found in six of the ten main cloud types (see opposite). Their presence is a reminder, to any who might forget, that the atmosphere around us is just as much an ocean as is the sea below.

Top: over Castagneto Carducci, Tuscany, Italy, by Katrin Pfeifer (Member 12533)

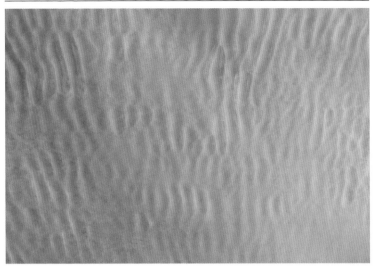

Like ripples in the sand: Cirrocumulus undulatus.

CLOUD-COLLECTING POINTS:

○ 20 points: Any undulatus

○ 10 points: Bonus for undulations at more than one level, giving a crisscrossed effect (see duplicatus, p. 46)

+ Add Total To Page 5

Variety is found in: Stratus (p. 16), Stratocumulus (p. 12), Altocumulus (p. 18), Altostratus (p. 20), Cirrocumulus (p. 24), Cirrostratus (p. 26), noctilucent (p. 98).

○ *I spotted undulatus*

DATE   TIME

LOCATION

WEATHER CONDITIONS

IMAGE FILE NAME(S)

Lacunosus

Hole size varies from low Stratocumulus *(top)* to high Cirrocumulus *(bottom)*.

A rare, fleeting formation, the lacunosus variety is identified in terms of the gaps between cloud elements, rather than the clouds themselves. It is when a cloud layer is composed of more or less regular holes, around which fringes of cloud form, like a net or rough honeycomb.

Even though lacunosus forms at all three *cloud levels*, it is an elusive prize for any cloud collector, since it is so short-lived. Like the equally transient pileus cloud (page 50), lacunosus therefore earns considerable cloud-collecting points.

The holes of this variety are formed by sinking pockets of air, and the cloud fringes around them by air rising up between the pockets to replace them. Such sinking can occur when a layer of cooler air finds itself over a warmer one. Being more dense, the cooler air sinks down through the warmer air. The appearance is similar to the rough honeycomb pattern you occasionally see on the surface of a hot cup of tea. As the tea on the surface cools and contracts, it sinks in pockets through the hotter tea below, which bubbles up in between to replace it. That said, no one is completely sure why sometimes the cool air sinks to form lacunosus, while other times the warm air rises in pockets to form the opposite arrangement of *cloudlets* with gaps between (such as the one on page 19).

A crater-pocked landscape, courtesy of Altocumulus lacunosus cloud holes.

CLOUD-COLLECTING POINTS:

○ 40 points: Any lacunosus

○ 35 points: Bonus for when you spot the rarer lacunosus among the unruly form of Stratocumulus

+ Add Total To Page 5

Variety is found in: Stratocumulus (p. 12), Altocumulus (p. 18), Cirrocumulus (p. 24), noctilucent (p. 98).

Don't confuse with: fallstreak holes (p. 84).

○ *I spotted lacunosus*

DATE

TIME

LOCATION

WEATHER CONDITIONS

IMAGE FILE NAME(S)

Radiatus

Cumulus radiatus, or "cloud streets."

When a layer of cloud rolls or clumps extends in long lines that stretch off to the horizon, the effect of perspective makes these lines converge, like railway tracks, toward a point. Such a formation is a variety known as radiatus, and it can be found at all three *cloud levels*.

The parallel cloud lines form along the direction of the wind at cloud level. When they form perpendicular to the wind, they are of the undulatus variety (page 42), rather than radiatus.

Radiatus in low Cumulus clouds (page 10) are known as "cloud streets." These formations cause glider pilots to wet themselves with excitement, for they indicate avenues of lifting air along which the pilots can reliably gain altitude.

When it comes to high, ice-crystal clouds, the most dramatic examples of radiatus result from jet streams—the ribbons of 180 mph winds that encircle the globe in the midlatitudes at the top of the *troposphere*. Known as "jet-stream Cirrus" (see opposite), these radiatus varieties of Cirrus (page 22) can be spread over great distances by the high winds. Occasionally they appear to extend all the way from one horizon right overhead to the opposite one. The perspective causes the cloud rows to bulge dramatically above, while converging at "radiation points" on each horizon. Such an impressive radiatus formation will be a source of great pride for any cloud collector but it is practically impossible to photograph in its entirety, since it stretches over such a large part of the sky.

Over the Bahamas by Paul Cooper (Member 1523)

Either "jet-stream Cirrus" or contrails left from an amazing Blue Angels fly-by.

CLOUD-COLLECTING POINTS:

○ 35 points: Any radiatus

○ 30 points: Bonus for jet-stream Cirrus, or Cirrus radiatus, that extends overhead, from horizon to horizon

+ Add Total To Page 5

○ *I spotted radiatus*

Variety is found in: Cumulus (p. 10), Stratocumulus (p. 12), Altocumulus (p. 18), Altostratus (p. 20), Cirrus (p. 22).

Don't confuse with: undulatus (p. 42)—perpendicular to wind at cloud level.

DATE   TIME

LOCATION

WEATHER CONDITIONS

IMAGE FILE NAME(S)

Duplicatus

The light and shade of a low Sun can reveal Altostratus duplicatus layers.

Some clouds earn substantial collecting points because they are rare, and others just because they are very difficult to identify. It is the latter case for the variety duplicatus, in which a layered cloud occurs at two altitudes at the same time.

When duplicatus occurs in the low Stratocumulus cloud (page 12), which contains water droplets rather than ice crystals, the lower of the two layers is usually too thick to see through, and so obscures the higher one. It is possible to notice that the cloud is divided into two layers only when the higher one appears through gaps in the lower. And, truth be told, in this low cloud, it's not a sight worth getting excited about. You might think the same could be said for duplicatus varieties in Altocumulus (page 18) and Altostratus (page 20), but then these midlevel clouds can be rather less opaque. So when the Sun is very low in the sky, the duplicatus formation can become visible as the lower of the two layers is darkened by the Earth's shadow, while the higher is bathed in ruby hues. In fact, Altocumulus duplicatus can produce the most gloriously prolonged sunsets.

In the high Cirrus (page 22) and Cirrostratus (page 26) clouds, you can most readily identify the split layers of duplicatus when they happen to have the filaments of the fibratus species (page 38). The fibers of each layer can point different ways with differing wind directions at each altitude. Since these clouds are made of ice crystals and so are generally semi-transparent, the layers appear as one, with a beautiful cross-hatched pattern.

Over Stratfield Mortimer, Berkshire, UK by Stephen Burt (Member 2814)

Differing wind directions reveal this Cirrostratus fibratus cloud to be in two layers.

CLOUD-COLLECTING POINTS:

O 25 points: Any duplicatus

O 15 points: Bonus for when the duplicatus variety is revealed in Altocumulus by a long-lasting sunrise or sunset

+ Add Total To Page 5

Variety is found in: Stratocumulus (p. 12), Altocumulus (p. 18), Altostratus (p. 20), Cirrus (p. 22), Cirrostratus (p. 26).

Don't confuse with: two different genera, e.g., Cirrostratus (p. 26) over Stratus (p. 16).

O *I spotted duplicatus*

DATE   TIME

LOCATION

WEATHER CONDITIONS

IMAGE FILE NAME(S)

Pileus

Pileus clouds are the comb-over hairstyle of the cloud world.

The most short-lived of all the *accessory clouds*, pileus is also the most beautiful. It shares much in common with lenticularis (page 34) and cap clouds (page 72), which form when a *stable airstream* rises to pass over raised ground. In the case of pileus, however, the obstacle is not rocky terrain, but something altogether more ephemeral—another cloud.

Pileus looks rather like a smooth, white beret, or, perhaps, a Donald-Trump comb-over hairstyle. It is a horizontal cap cloud that appears momentarily on top of the crisp, cauliflower summit of a Cumulus congestus (page 10), or the softer one of a young Cumulonimbus (page 30). Pileus can appear as one of these large *convection clouds* develops upward and encounters a moist stable airstream blowing above. This is forced to rise by the vigorous currents surging up the center of the cloud below, cooling it just enough for some of its moisture to condense into droplets. These evaporate as the airflow sinks back down again past the convection cloud.

A pileus earns high points for the cloud collector because, unlike its relation, velum (page 52), it never hangs around for long. Cloudspotters have to be sharp-eyed to add one to their collection. The vigorous convection cloud that made it inevitably continues its rise, pushing its bald head through the hairstyle. Donald Trump's head will eventually do the same.

This is officially known as a "fancy" pileus. (Actually, it's not; it's just a pileus.)

CLOUD-COLLECTING POINTS:

○ 45 points: Any pileus

○ 15 points: Bonus for one that forms over the top of a Cumulus congestus cloud that looks like Donald Trump

+ Add Total To Page 5

Normally found in the company of: Cumulus congestus (p. 10), Cumulonimbus (p. 30).

Don't confuse with: lenticularis (p. 34), cap clouds (p. 72).

○ *I spotted pileus*

DATE   TIME

LOCATION

WEATHER CONDITIONS

IMAGE FILE NAME(S)

Velum

Velum is the thin, horizontal strip of cloud in front of the Cumulus congestus.

Velum is an *accessory cloud* that turns up in the same sort of places as the pileus cloud (page 50). Though they form in a similar way, they have quite different natures. Unfortunately for velum, it is usually the less attractive and more ponderous of the pair.

Velum is Latin for ship's sail. This name is a tad misleading for it is a thin horizontal patch of cloud, rather than one that hangs down from a tall mast and catches the wind. You'll spot a velum cloud either just above or around the sides of a group of large *convection clouds,* such as Cumulus congestus (see page 10) or Cumulonimbus (page 30). Observed from a distance, the velum usually looks like a white or grey strip that can be separate from, or mixed in with, the convection clouds.

While the smaller pileus appears locally over individual convection clouds, velum is often spread over a very large area. If the cloud layer was not already around before the convection clouds grew up through it, the velum can sometimes have resulted from the tops of Cumulus clouds spreading out upon reaching a layer of *stable air* above. When, later, more powerful Cumulus clouds finally burst through the stable air layer, the velum remains loitering at their flanks for some time.

Over Teruel, Spain, by Luis Antonio Gil Pellín (Member 14194)

Forming in a stable layer, velum can linger long after the convection clouds have gone.

CLOUD-COLLECTING POINTS:

○ 15 points: Any velum

○ 10 points: Bonus for when you notice it still hanging around after the convection clouds have dissipated

+ Add Total To Page 5

Normally found in the company of:
a group of Cumulus congestus (p. 10) or Cumulonimbus (p. 30).

Don't confuse with: pileus (p. 50).

○ *I spotted velum*

DATE   TIME

LOCATION

WEATHER CONDITIONS

IMAGE FILE NAME(S)

Pannus

An ominous sky is always made a little more ominous by pannus clouds.

Don't get too excited about adding pannus to your cloud collection. When you do spot one, you're likely to be rather underwhelmed, for they aren't good-lookers.

Loitering in the saturated atmosphere just below rain clouds, they resemble some sort of cloud version of hooligans, killing time outside McDonald's on a Saturday night.

These dark shreds of cloud, strictly classified as Stratus fractus (see page 16), give the sky a threatening air. The atmosphere below a precipitating cloud can become very humid, on account of all the moisture falling through it. Only the slightest rising gust can then cool the air enough for some of this moisture to condense into tiny droplets, which hang around as wisps of thin cloud.

If it is not raining or snowing when you notice dark shreds of pannus below a forbidding sky, you can be confident that it will be very soon. Pannus are the five-minute-precipitation warning of the cloud world.

As with loitering groups of teens, the sinister appearance of pannus clouds owes a lot to their surroundings. The shreds of cloud need only be thick enough to block a little light for our eyes to register them as darker than the thick, dark rain clouds above. Away from their precipitous context, pannus would be seen for the weedy wisps that they are. The same could be said of the prepubescent fourteen-year-olds, once stripped of their crew and ubiquitous hoods.

Over Stratfield Mortimer, Berkshire, UK, by Stephen Burt (Member 2814)

Is that a punk kid brandishing a 40? No, it's a pannus in moisture-laden air.

CLOUD-COLLECTING POINTS:

○ 10 points: Any pannus

○ 10 points: Bonus for correctly predicting to your companion that it will rain within five minutes, and being right

+ Add Total To Page 5

○ *I spotted pannus*

Normally found in the company of: Cumulus congestus (p. 10), Cumulonimbus (p. 30), Nimbostratus (p. 28).

Don't confuse with: Cumulus fractus (p. 10) beneath Altostratus (p. 20).

DATE   TIME

LOCATION

WEATHER CONDITIONS

IMAGE FILE NAME(S)

Mamma

Mamma under a Cumulonimbus anvil.

"What on Earth are those?" is the usual reaction when people see photographs of mamma clouds. Also known as "'mammatus," these *supplementary features* hang down from a layer of cloud in smooth or rough pouches that often have the appearance of udders (which is what "mamma" means in Latin).

With such an otherworldly, *Independence Day* appearance, mamma are a must-have for any cloud collection. They can be found on a whole range of cloud types (see opposite), but the most dramatic examples occur on the underside of the huge anvils known as incus (page 70), that spread out at the top of mature Cumulonimbus storm clouds (page 30) and can cover all the visible sky.

Some claim that mamma are harbingers of stormy weather, and what with the association between these pendulous cloud-boobs and Cumulonimbus, you might think they have a point. But mamma tend to form at the rear, rather than the front, of storms. Once you see mamma formations above you, the storm has usually passed over, or missed you entirely.

Each lobe of mamma is typically one to two miles across, and appears for around ten minutes. There are several theories about why they form, but an extensive 2006 scientific review of all the studies to date concluded that no one's really sure.

Above: As the underside of its anvil reveals, this Cumulonimbus needs milking.
Next page: It's hard to spot mamma in Cirrus.

CLOUD-COLLECTING POINTS:

○ 30 points: Any mamma

○ 25 points: Bonus for when you're far
enough away to see mamma under a
Cumulonimbus anvil (pp. 30, 70)

+ Add Total To Page 5

Normally found in the company of:
Stratocumulus (p. 12), Altocumulus
(p. 18), Altostratus (p. 20), Cirrus
(p. 22), Cirrocumulus (p. 24),
Cumulonimbus (p. 30), contrails
(p. 78), pyrocumulus (p. 80).

○ *I spotted mamma*

DATE   TIME

LOCATION

WEATHER CONDITIONS

IMAGE FILE NAME(S)

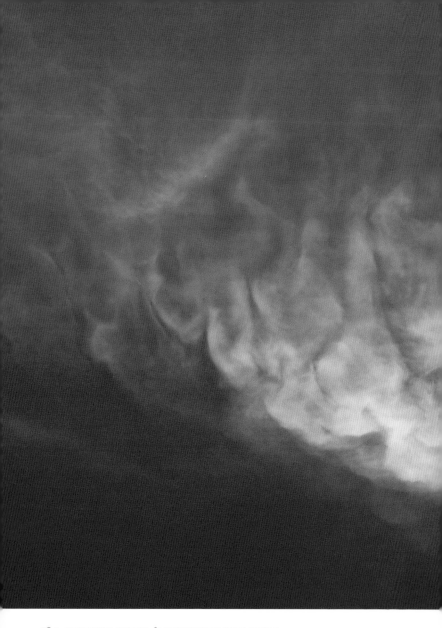

Virga

When wind speeds vary considerably with height, virga can have abrupt corners.

When you look up to find jellyfish floating above, you are either diving or beneath the cloud *supplementary feature* known as virga.

In essence, this is just a cloud raining or snowing, but with one important difference: the precipitation never reaches the ground. If the droplets or ice crystals (or anything between the two) fall through air that is warm enough and/or dry enough, they can evaporate before ever landing.

The appearance of virga from the ground is of trails that hang down like tentacles from clumps of cloud, waving not in the currents of the ocean, but in those of the lower atmosphere. When virga occur below low-level clouds, they are composed of water droplets, and appear grey. When they consist of ice crystals, having fallen from midlevel or high-level clouds, they have a much paler appearance. But beware: This distinction is a tenuous one, because our eyes judge color and tone relative to the brightness of the background. The same trail of virga can appear whiter or greyer depending on the sky behind. Fallstreak holes (page 84) are specific cases of virga falling from a layer of *supercooled droplets* to leave behind a hole.

When a cloud's precipitation can be seen to reach all the way to the ground, it is no longer called virga, but "praecipitatio."

Above: Virga is rain or snow that evaporates before reaching the ground.
Next page: Varied wind speeds can also make virga very slanted.

CLOUD-COLLECTING POINTS:

○ 25 points: Any virga

○ 15 points: Bonus for when the virga trail falls through an abrupt change of wind and develops a sharp corner

+ Add Total To Page 5

Normally found in the company of:
Cumulus (p. 10), Stratocumulus (p. 12), Altocumulus (p. 18), Altostratus (p. 20), Cirrocumulus (p. 24), Nimbostratus (p. 28).

Don't confuse with: Cirrus (p. 22).

○ *I spotted virga*

DATE   TIME

LOCATION

WEATHER CONDITIONS

IMAGE FILE NAME(S)

Arcus

The horizontally extended form of arcus, known as a shelf cloud.

Storm chasers tend to have an abundance of arcus in their cloud collections, for this *supplementary feature* is rather like the front bumper of a storm cloud—a long, dark, horizontal roll or shelf running along the base of the storm cloud's front edge (around the registration plate). So arcus is the first cloud feature to arrive as the storm runs you over.

Like those other brute-cloud groupies, tuba (page 68) and incus (page 70), arcus hang out only in the company of hefty Cumulus congestus (page 10) or Cumulonimbus (page 30) clouds or those most brutish of all cloud systems, the fierce *multicell* and *supercell storms*. Arcus forms as the cold air that is dragged down by all the precipitation falling within storm clouds splays out upon reaching the ground. As it spreads around the storm, it burrows under the warmer, less-dense air at ground level. This is lifted most forcefully in the direction of the cloud's movement, forming a "gust front," in which the warmer air's moisture can condense into water droplets that appear as arcus.

Sometimes, arcus can protrude forward from the storm as a dark, ragged ledge, known as a "shelf cloud." More rarely, the lifting motion can cause a wave of rising and falling air that races ahead of the storm, the arcus appearing as a roll cloud (page 82), which rotates within the wave as it travels.

Above: Arcus is like the front bumper of a speeding storm cloud.
Next page: An arcus.

CLOUD-COLLECTING POINTS:

○ 30 points: Any arcus

○ 25 points: Bonus for one that clearly protrudes out in a ledge, which is known as a shelf cloud

+ Add Total To Page 5

Normally found with: large Cumulus congestus (p. 10), Cumulonimbus (p. 30) and multicell or supercell storms.

Don't confuse with: "wall clouds" in the rising air at the back end of storms.

○ *I spotted arcus*

DATE   TIME

LOCATION

WEATHER CONDITIONS

IMAGE FILE NAME(S)

Tuba

The first tentative signs of a cloud finger.

The air below a storm cloud is often a wild confusion of blustery, gusty and not-at-all-tranquil winds. But when the storm develops from a single Cumulonimbus cloud (page 30) into a coordinated system, known as a *multicell* or *supercell storm,* the mêlée of air currents becomes much more organized. This is when a tuba can form.

Resembling a cloud finger descending from the storm's base, the tuba forms in the air sucked upward into the storm to feed its vigorous vertical growth. Like an upside-down version of bath water going down the drain, the rising air can start rotating in a vortex. In a big storm cell, the rapidly rising air expands and cools enough for some of its moisture to condense to form the walls of the tuba. Also known as a "funnel cloud," it can be the birth of a tornado.

A tuba can also form when the air is not rising but sinking from the base of individual clouds, such as Cumulus congestus (page 10) and Cumulo-nimbus. Dragged toward the ground by the cloud's heavy showers, this sinking air can cause vortices to form. These are rarely as violent as the upward ones, so tubas are less pronounced. They herald not tornadoes, but the less ferocious landspouts or waterspouts.

Whatever a tuba is heralding, keep your distance when adding it to your cloud collection—just in case it has a mind to add a cloudspotter to its own collection of flying debris.

Over Castle Rock, Colorado, US, by Jim Karanik (Member 12842)

A waterspout is when a tuba touches down on an expanse of water.

CLOUD-COLLECTING POINTS:

○ 35 points: Any tuba

○ 25 points: Bonus for when the vortex of air becomes so vigorous that the tuba extends to the ground

+ Add Total To Page 5

Normally found in the company of: individual Cumulus congestus (p. 10) and Cumulonimbus (p. 30), but most prominently at the inflow of huge multicell and supercell storm systems.

○ *I spotted tuba*

DATE	TIME

LOCATION

WEATHER CONDITIONS

IMAGE FILE NAME(S)

Incus

You have to be a long way away to be able to see a storm cloud's incus.

An incus is a part of a Cumulonimbus cloud (page 30). In fact, it is the most distinctive feature of the storm cloud: the huge canopy of ice crystals that spreads out at its top. Often covering hundreds of square miles, it is much larger than any of the other *supplementary features*, and gives a mature storm cloud the distinctive shape of a blacksmith's anvil (the meaning of incus in Latin).

Why does an incus form? One minute the cloud is growing upward, building from a Cumulus congestus tower (see page 10), its summit softening as the droplets there freeze into ice crystals, and the next it starts spreading out in all directions. The vigorous vertical development of an enormous storm cloud is blocked, and it is forced to splay out, when it encounters what meteorologists call a *temperature inversion*.

On average, air becomes colder the higher you go through the lower atmosphere. But only on average. Often, a situation occurs when a region of warmer air blows over the top of a colder one. Such an inversion of the normal temperature profile tends to act as an invisible ceiling to the growth of clouds. All of a sudden, the warmer air within the cloud is no longer warmer, and so less dense, than the air around. So it stops floating upward. The inversion that causes the top of a Cumulonimbus to spread as incus is usually the one marking the boundary between the *troposphere* and the *stratosphere*. Called the *tropopause*, it's where the air temperature no longer falls with altitude, and may even begin to rise.

Over Llanos de Gea, Teruel, Spain, by Luis Antonio Gil Pellín (Member 14194)

It's not Armageddon over Austin, Texas—just the incus of a Cumulonimbus.

CLOUD-COLLECTING POINTS:

○ 20 points: Any incus

○ 15 points: Bonus for when this canopy of ice crystals has a ribbed or streaked appearance

+ Add Total To Page 5

Normally found in the company of: Cumulonimbus (p. 30).

Don't confuse with: the mushroom cloud of a nuclear explosion.

○ *I Spotted incus*

DATE   TIME

LOCATION

WEATHER CONDITIONS

IMAGE FILE NAME(S)

Cap & Banner

A banner cloud.

While cap and banner clouds form in slightly different ways, they share the distinction of being clouds that hang out around mountain summits.

When a cap cloud forms, it tends to look like a hat, perched upon the mountain's head. Sometimes it looks like a humble skullcap. Other times, it splays out in a full mother-in-law-at-a-wedding extravaganza. Occasionally, the mountain seems to be wearing one hat on top of another, which is surely a mountain fashion faux pas. Whichever it is, a cap cloud forms as a *stable airstream* rises to pass over a peak, cooling as it does so. It is a particular example of a lenticularis *species* (page 34), in which the cloud lies over the mountaintop, rather than downwind from it.

Banner clouds form in the same places as cap clouds, but look more as if the mountain is letting its hair flow in the wind, and they form in a slightly different way from cap clouds. As a stiff wind blows over a pronounced high peak, the air pressure drops slightly behind the peak. This can cool the air enough for its moisture to condense briefly into droplets or ice crystals.

Cloudspotters should be careful not to add the wrong cloud to their collections. Clouds such as Stratus (page 16) or Stratocumulus (page 12) clinging to mountaintops won't do. Only a jaunty cloud hat or a mane of mountain hair earns the points.

Above: A cap cloud, known to some as a pink-fluffy-bobble-hat cloud.
Next page: The mother-in-law-at-a-wedding cap cloud.

CLOUD-COLLECTING POINTS:

O 30 points: Cap or banner cloud

O 20 points: Bonus for a cap in layers (above) or a banner cloud showing turbulent whirls (opposite)

+ Add Total To Page 5

Typical altitudes: around, or just above, a mountain summit.

Precipitation: from cap (but rare).

Don't confuse with: pileus (p. 50), Stratus (p. 16) or Stratocumulus (p. 12).

O *I spotted a cap or banner cloud*

DATE   TIME

LOCATION

WEATHER CONDITIONS

IMAGE FILE NAME(S)

Kelvin-Helmholtz

The breaking waves can appear in Stratocumulus *(top)* and Cirrus *(bottom)*.

The Kelvin-Helmholtz wave cloud scores the highest number of points of all the clouds. Looking just like enormous waves breaking on the shore, it is rare, fleeting and the favorite of cloudspotting surfers. A well-defined Kelvin-Helmholtz is the crown jewel in many a cloud collection, for it requires the cloud-spotter to be blessed with eagle-eyed sky awareness and sheer blind luck. In one spotting alone, this cloud can help observers overtake their fiercest cloud-collecting rivals.

It appears at all three *cloud levels,* and can be thought of as a very specific example of the undulatus cloud *variety* (page 42), tending to be found in Stratocumulus (page 12), Altocumulus (page 18) or Cirrus (page 22) clouds. It can also sometimes be seen along the top edge of a layer of fog (page 90). In all cases, the formation lasts for no more than a minute or two.

The distinctive breaking-wave appearance is caused by wind shear. When cloud develops at an abrupt boundary between layers of colder air below and warmer air above, and the upper layer is moving more rapidly than the lower one, undulations can develop along its surface. If there is enough shearing, these can roll up into a succession of vortices. They may look like a surfer's idea of heaven, but the mechanism is in fact quite different from that of ocean waves breaking in shallow water.

Top: over Gent, Belgium, by Frits Kuitenbrouwer (Member 13684)

Enormous breakers on a calm sea: Kelvin-Helmholtz clouds in thick Cirrus.

CLOUD-COLLECTING POINTS:

○ 55 points: Any Kelvin-Helmholtz

○ 30 points: Bonus for when the Kelvin-Helmholtz appears along the top of a lenticularis cloud (p. 32)

+ Add Total To Page 5

Typical altitudes: from ground level (in fog) to 40,000 ft.

Precipitation: influence is not significant.

Don't confuse with: regular waves of undulatus (p. 42) that aren't breaking.

○ *I Spotted Kelvin-Helmholtz*

DATE   TIME

LOCATION

WEATHER CONDITIONS

IMAGE FILE NAME(S)

Contrails

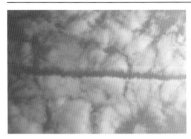

A distrail, short for dissipation trail.

Before the start of the First World War and the advent of high-altitude flight, our skies appeared very different from the way they do today—there were no condensation trails, or contrails, which form in the exhaust of aircraft.

There's no confusing these man-made clouds with the natural ones. Following the aircraft's path, contrails tend to appear as long, straight slashes of white across the blue. In the vicinity of airports, however, they can sometimes form large loops, due to the stacking formation of aircraft waiting to land.

The length of time contrails remain in the sky—or indeed whether they form at all—varies greatly depending on the air conditions up at cruising altitude. When it's cold enough and moist enough, the *water vapor* contained in the plane's hot exhaust gases mixes with the very cold air to condense and form ice crystals. In some conditions, these soon evaporate. In others, they can persist for hours, the ice crystals absorbing water vapor from the surrounding air to grow in size and spread out in the high winds. In this way, contrails often encourage the formation of Cirrus (page 22), Cirrocumulus (page 24) and Cirrostratus (page 26) ice-crystal clouds.

Bonus cloud-collecting points are awarded for spotting a distrail. The opposite of a contrail, this is when a plane cuts out a gap as it flies through a cloud layer. This happens when the heat and turbulence of its engine make the cloud droplets evaporate, or when it introduces *icing nuclei* that encourage the cloud's *supercooled droplets* to freeze and fall below.

Over Sint-Pieters-Rode, Belgium, by Guy Lorent (Member 12976)

Aircraft contrails—a nightmare for anyone shooting a period drama outside.

CLOUD-COLLECTING POINTS:

○ 10 points: Any contrail

○ 10 points: Bonus for when the plane cuts a gap out of an existing layer of cloud to form a distrail

+ Add Total To Page 5

Typical altitudes: 28,000-40,000 ft.

Precipitation: none.

Don't confuse with: too straight to be mistaken for other clouds.

○ *I spotted a contrail*

DATE   TIME

LOCATION

WEATHER CONDITIONS

IMAGE FILE NAME(S)

Pyrocumulus

Forest-fire smoke can have a reddish tinge, while pyrocumulus clouds can appear dark grey **(top)** or bright white **(bottom)** depending on which side of the cloud the sunlight falls.

When clouds form in columns of air floating up from forest fires, they are known as pyrocumulus. Anything that is hot enough to produce strong *convection currents* can give rise to clouds if there is enough moisture around. Fierce forest fires and large volcanic eruptions can lead to pyrocumulus clouds that are large enough to produce lightning or tuba cloud features (page 68), which lead to landspouts or waterspouts. Pyrocumulus also form over the towers of power stations, when they are sometimes known as "fumulus." This is one of the few man-made clouds—another being contrails (page 78).

Forest fires, volcanoes and power stations not only provide the heat needed to form these clouds, but they also introduce countless microscopic particles into the air that act as *condensation nuclei*, on which the cloud's droplets can form. This means pyrocumulus droplets tend to be very small and plentiful, making the cloud appear thick—especially when mixed with ash or smoke.

Man-made pyrocumulus, also known as "fumulus."

CLOUD-COLLECTING POINTS:

○ 10 points: Any pyrocumulus

○ 25 points: Bonus for one that is so vigorous it leads to thunder and lightning

+ Add Total To Page 5

Typical altitudes: 0–5,000 ft.

Precipitation: rain possible if grows very large over volcanoes/forest fires.

Don't confuse with: smoke or volcanic ash alone, without any cloud.

○ *I spotted pyrocumulus*

DATE   TIME

LOCATION

WEATHER CONDITIONS

IMAGE FILE NAME(S)

Roll Cloud

Top and bottom: Roll clouds can move ahead of big storms that are dissipating.

This is a long, low tube of cloud, which can appear to extend horizontally from horizon to horizon. Sometimes a roll cloud has a very smooth, silky surface. At other times, it can appear quite rough and bumpy. Roll clouds can move at speeds of up to 35 mph, with the tube appearing to rotate as it rolls along. The direction of rotation is not as it would be for a solid tube rolling along the ground. In fact, the roll cloud rotates against its direction of travel—the cloud surface lifting at the front and dropping down at the back.

One famous roll cloud, "Morning Glory," appears in Northern Queensland, Australia. This forms in a solitary wave of air and is caused by colliding sea breezes over the Cape York Peninsula. But most roll clouds are types of arcus (page 64), and are caused by storms. As the storm dissipates, gusting winds of cold air can continue to spread out ahead of it, and form a roll of cloud that separates away from the rest of the storm.

Top: over Collinsville Oklahoma, US by Indie Justice (Member 14210)

The queen of roll clouds is Australia's "Morning Glory."

CLOUD-COLLECTING POINTS:

○ 30 points: Any roll cloud

○ 10 points: Bonus for when the roll cloud passes right over you, and you stop what you are doing to watch it

+ Add Total To Page 5

Typical altitudes: 1,000–5,000 ft.

Precipitation: none itself, but it can be associated with storms.

Don't confuse with: other forms of arcus (p. 64) attached to storm clouds.

○ *I spotted a roll cloud*

DATE

TIME

LOCATION

WEATHER CONDITIONS

IMAGE FILE NAME(S)

Fallstreak Hole

They look bizarre, but fallstreak holes are not actually that rare. Also called "hole-punch clouds," they are crisp gaps in midlevel or high-level cloud layers, below which dangle trails of ice crystals.

To form a fallstreak hole, the cloud layer must consist of *supercooled droplets*—when its water is in liquid form despite temperatures at cloud level being well below 32 degrees F. This is actually quite common, for pure water suspended as droplets in the air behaves very differently from tap water in the freezer. If there aren't enough of the right sort of tiny particles in the atmosphere to act as *icing nuclei*, onto which they can start to freeze, droplets remain liquid until temperatures drop to around -40 degrees F. They "want" to freeze, but can only do so when there are seeds on which the crystals can begin to grow.

A fallstreak hole forms when one region of the cloud finally starts to freeze and begins a chain reaction. All the moisture from the supercooled droplets in the area rushes to join the ice crystals, which quickly grow big enough to fall below. A form of virga (page 60), the trail of ice crystals doesn't tend to reach the ground, but evaporates before getting that far.

What starts the freezing? Sometimes it's ice crystals falling into the cloud's droplets from a higher Cirrus cloud (page 22). At other times, it is caused by the exhaust of a plane climbing or descending through the cloud to form a "distrail" (see page 78). Particles in the exhaust act as icing nuclei that start the freezing.

Above: Once some droplets freeze, they rob others of moisture and start to descend.
Next page: A cigar-shaped fallstreak hole, caused by a plane climbing through the cloud.

CLOUD-COLLECTING POINTS:

○ 35 points: Any fallstreak hole

○ 15 points: Bonus for when the trail of ice crystals has iridescent colors (p. 102) as the Sun shines through it

+ Add Total To Page 5

Typical altitudes: 6,500–20,000 ft.

Precipitation: the crystals evaporate before reaching the ground.

Don't confuse with: Cirrus (p. 22).

○ *I spotted a fallstreak hole*

DATE

TIME

LOCATION

WEATHER CONDITIONS

IMAGE FILE NAME(S)

Next page: over Duxford, Cambridgeshire, UK, by Rachel Summers (Member 9892)

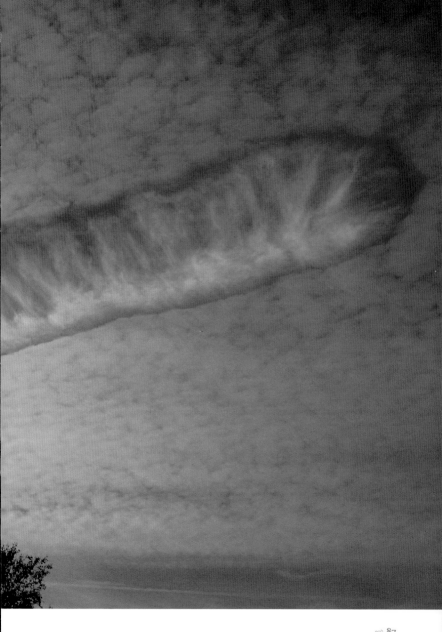

Horseshoe Vortex

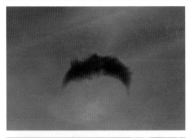

Had the French named it, this would surely be called the "croissant cloud."

What a subtle little wisp of cloud the horseshoe vortex is! It is easily missed by anyone other than the most keen-eyed cloudspotters, intent on adding it to their collection. The rare and fleeting horseshoe vortex cloud appears for just a minute or so before evaporating. Anyone lucky enough to spot one must take a photo if they want to be believed by their cloud-collecting friends.

This cloud forms in a region of rotating air, or vortex. While the familiar orientation for a vortex is vertical (see tuba, page 68), it can occasionally develop on a horizontal axis. This is when the gently rotating crescent of the horseshoe vortex cloud can form. The movement of air seems to result from an updraft that is sent into a spin when it reaches a sudden change in the horizontal winds above. Rarely are conditions right for a cloud to appear within the vortex, but, when they are, the air in the upper arc of the vortex cools enough to develop a rotating crescent of cloud. One of the best places to spot horseshoe vortex clouds is in the vicinity of *supercell storms*. The winds rushing in to feed the storm's growth can lead to just the right sort of shearing air currents.

This beautiful little cloud may not lead to any precipitation, but it will rain down luck upon anyone fortunate enough to spot it—as well as impressive cloud-collecting points.

Top: over Jasper, Alberta, Canada, by Eric Rehwald (Member 14215)

An upside-down horseshoe, considered unlucky by some, but never by cloudspotters.

CLOUD-COLLECTING POINTS:

○ 50 points: Any horseshoe vortex

○ 20 points: Bonus for managing to catch it on film, so that you can see the way the winds make it rotate

+ Add Total To Page 5

Typical altitudes: 2,000–5,000 ft.

Precipitation: not from this snippet, but it does often form in the vicinity of large storm clouds.

Don't confuse with: unmistakable!

○ *I spotted a horseshoe vortex*

DATE   TIME

LOCATION

WEATHER CONDITIONS

IMAGE FILE NAME(S)

Fog & Mist

Steam fog can form over a lake.

The distinction between fog and mist relates to visibility. Officially, you can see 1-2 kilometers in mist but no more than 1 kilometer in fog—one's just a thicker version of the other. Though fog is sometimes described as ground-level Stratus cloud (page 16), since that's the lowest of the main clouds, it often forms quite differently.

Fog appears if air is cooled enough by its proximity to the ground or water surface for its moisture to condense into droplets. There are two main ways this cooling can happen.

"Radiation fog" forms after long, cold and clear nights. With no blanket of cloud cover to keep the warmth in, the ground quickly radiates the day's warmth into the night sky, and can cool the air enough to form droplets. On higher ground, the cold, foggy air can sink downhill and gather as "valley fog."

"Advection fog" occurs when air cools as it blows over a warmer surface to a colder one. If these are ocean surfaces, it's called "sea fog." Then there's "steam fog"—when cold air blows over warmer water, such as a lake, and the *water vapor* that evaporates off the surface instantly cools to form droplets.

That's not the end of it. There's also "upslope fog," "hill fog," "ice fog" (see page 94), "haar" and "frontal fog." No matter which one it is, cloudspotters will never get closer to a cloud than when they're enveloped in fog or mist.

Above: Radiation fog forms below cloud-free skies on long, cold, damp nights.
Next page: Valley fog seen from the hillside.

CLOUD-COLLECTING POINTS:

○ 15 points: Any fog or mist

○ 5 points: Bonus for crepuscular rays (p. 108) appearing in the fog as the sunlight begins to cast shadows

+ Add Total To Page 5

Typical altitudes: ground/sea level.

Precipitation: "fog drip" moisture when droplets collide with solid surfaces.

Don't confuse with: airborne clouds, if you are the pilot of a plane.

○ *I spotted fog or mist*

DATE   TIME

LOCATION

WEATHER CONDITIONS

IMAGE FILE NAME(S)

Diamond Dust

Crystals of diamond dust sparkle as they tumble through the night air.

The sight of diamond dust glittering in the sunlight is unforgettable. A kind of fog made of ice crystals, it is often not thick enough to reduce visibility and its presence is then revealed only by the way the crystals glint in the light as they tumble through the air.

Diamond dust is sometimes also known as "ice fog," but this term tends to refer to a thicker ice-crystal fog that reduces visibility and consists of less regular crystal shapes. For classic diamond dust, temperatures need to be lower than about -40 degrees F. This means that the air's *water vapor* tends to collect directly as floating ice crystals, rather than condensing into droplets, which then freeze. The result is a ground-level version of a Cirrus (page 22) or Cirrostratus (page 26) cloud.

Such conditions are common in polar regions, particularly in the Antarctic, where the crystals grow very slowly, leading to diamond dust of regularly shaped little ice prisms. These do more than just glisten. By reflecting and *refracting* the light waves passing through, the crystals of diamond dust can produce extremely pure and extensive arcs, spots and rings of light, known as *halo phenomena* (see pages 120-131).

But cloudspotters needn't go to Antarctica to add these shimmering crystals to their cloud collection. Pure diamond dust, producing glorious halo phenomena, can also form downwind from ski-resort snow machines.

Over Apollo, Pennsylvania, US, by Grover Schrayer (Member 14209)

Halo phenomena can appear as the sun shines through diamond dust.

CLOUD-COLLECTING POINTS:

○ 30 points: Any diamond dust

○ 15 points: Bonus for when it scatters the sunlight to form a halo phenomenon (see pp. 120–131)

+ Add Total To Page 5

Typical altitude: ground level.

Precipitation: the tiny ice crystals are generally too few to gather significantly on the ground.

Don't confuse with: magic pixie dust.

○ *I Spotted diamond dust*

DATE   TIME

LOCATION

WEATHER CONDITIONS

IMAGE FILE NAME(S)

Nacreous

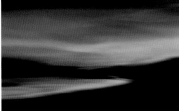

The hues of nacreous clouds change with the Sun's angle over the horizon.

Forming 10 to 20 miles up, in the *stratosphere*, at -121 degrees F, nacreous clouds show beautiful iridescent pastel hues as they scatter the light from the Sun when it is just below the horizon.

Sometimes called "mother-of-pearl clouds," their tiny, uniform ice crystals are very good at *diffracting* sunlight. This separates the light into bands of color, to create a much more dramatic version of the iridescence (page 102) sometimes seen in lower clouds.

Also known as "polar stratospheric clouds" since they tend to appear over higher-latitude regions of the world, nacreous clouds are like a stratospheric version of the lenticularis *species* of wave cloud (page 34). They form when the atmosphere is so *stable* that waves produced as air flows over mountains down at ground level are transferred up through the atmosphere, and push moisture into the lower stratosphere. The best time of year to spot them is in winter, when temperatures are lowest.

Sadly, these most mezmerising of clouds are also the most destructive for our environment. Their tiny ice crystals act as catalysts that speed up the destruction of the protective ozone layer by the CFC gases we've released into the atmosphere. For clouds to have such otherworldly beauty, there always has to be a catch.

Due to their height, nacreous can shine for as long as two hours after sunset.

CLOUD-COLLECTING POINTS:

○ 45 points: Any nacreous

○ 20 points: Bonus for watching through the sunset until it is no longer lit, and the colors suddenly switch off

+ Add Total To Page 5

Typical altitudes: 10-20 miles.

Precipitation: none.

Don't confuse with: iridescence (p. 102) that appears in much lower clouds within the troposphere.

○ *I spotted nacreous*

DATE   TIME

LOCATION

WEATHER CONDITIONS

IMAGE FILE NAME(S)

Noctilucent

The mysterious noctilucent clouds are higher than any other cloud in the atmosphere. Also known as "polar mesospheric clouds," they have an eerie, bluish-white appearance, often showing delicate ripples or billows.

Noctilucent clouds form in the *mesosphere,* at altitudes of 30 to 50 miles—almost at the limit of the atmosphere. Being so high means that, in the higher latitudes where they are most frequently seen, noctilucent clouds shine out against the night sky well after the Sun has dropped over the horizon. They still catch the sunlight when the rest of the sky is dark. Their name comes from Latin for "night shining."

Quite how noctilucent clouds form is by no means clear. The mesosphere is a region where air temperatures can be as low as -195 degrees F but there is very little moisture at all. No one knows why the ice crystals that make up this cloud arise in such a dry and remote part of the atmosphere.

Historically, noctilucent clouds have tended to be spotted at latitudes higher than 50 degrees during the summer months. It now seems that they are appearing over much larger regions of the world and more frequently. Some scientists have speculated that this change might be related to global warming.

The best times for cloudspotters to try to add noctilucent clouds to their collections is soon after sunset or before sunrise from May to August in the Northern Hemisphere, and November to March in the Southern Hemisphere.

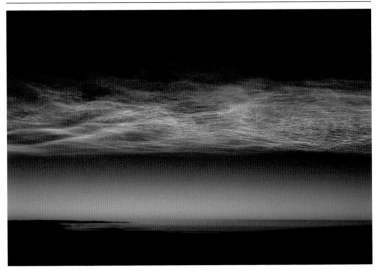

Above: Noctilucent clouds at the fringes of space, shot from a plane flying at 41,000 feet.
Next page: Ripples make the cloud look thicker and thinner when viewed from an angle.

CLOUD-COLLECTING POINTS:

○ 45 points: Any noctilucent

○ 20 points: Bonus if they're at latitudes below 50 degrees (south of Britain, north of the southern tip of New Zealand)

+ Add Total To Page 5

Typical altitudes: 30 to 50 miles.

Precipitation: from 50 miles up? No.

Don't confuse with: Cirrostratus (p. 26); no higher than 6 miles up, these are in shadow while noctilucent are still bright.

○ *I spotted noctilucent*

DATE   TIME

LOCATION

WEATHER CONDITIONS

IMAGE FILE NAME(S)

Iridescence

Cloud droplets form iridescence in pileus.

Iridescence is the beautiful effect of bands of pastel colors that can appear when sunlight or moonlight passes through thin clouds. Also known as "irisation," these mother-of-pearl colors are caused by the light being *diffracted* as it passes through the cloud. It is the same process that gives rise to colored discs around the Sun or Moon, called coronae (page 106). The light waves are dispersed as they pass around the cloud's tiny droplets or ice crystals, with different wavelengths being spread out by different amounts. Each wavelength can also produce an interference pattern of light and dark fringes. All this means that the sunlight is separated into alternating fringes of color.

Any thin cloud with droplets or ice crystals small and uniform enough can produce iridescent colors. Best viewed through sunglasses, the bands of pastel hues are reminiscent of those on oil slicks and can be seen over thin Stratocumulus (page 12), Altocumulus (page 18), Cirrocumulus (page 24) and Altostratus (page 20). Nacreous clouds (page 96) in the *stratosphere*, high above most weather clouds, show the most intense iridescence of all.

The colors can also appear at the edges of clouds thick enough to block much of the sunlight, such as lenticularis (page 34). To claim that every cloud has a silver lining is therefore wrong—some have tutti-frutti-colored ones.

Above: Iridescence can be produced by ice crystals, like those of this Cirrocumulus. *Next page:* Iridescence formed by cloud droplets in Altocumulus.

CLOUD-COLLECTING POINTS:

○ 20 points: Iridescence in any cloud except nacreous (p. 96)

○ 10 points: Bonus for when it gives a cloud a multicolored lining

+ Add Total To Page 5

Seen in: thin Stratocumulus (p. 12), Altostratus (p. 20), Altocumulus (p. 18), Cirrocumulus (p. 24), lenticularis (p. 34), and pileus (p. 50) edges.

Don't confuse with: glory (p. 110).

○ *I spotted iridescence*

DATE   TIME

LOCATION

WEATHER CONDITIONS

IMAGE FILE NAME(S)

Corona

Cirrostratus corona around the Sun *(top)* and the Moon *(bottom)*.

Look toward the Sun shining through thin cloud and you might find that it is surrounded by a corona. This is a bluish-white disc of light with a ruddy outer edge, often surrounded by rings of iridescent colors. Cloudspotters should be careful to protect their eyes by blocking the Sun with a hand. Coronae can be seen less painfully when clouds drift in front of a bright moon.

Closely related to cloud iridescence (page 102), coronae are caused when the light is *diffracted* as it passes around a cloud's particles. Only if these are all very small and the cloud layer is thin will the colors of the corona appear distinct around the central bright disc. The smaller the cloud droplets, the larger the corona.

Cloudspotters should take care not to confuse a corona with a 22° halo (page 120). Not only is the corona much smaller (the outer edge usually being less than 5 degrees from the Sun or Moon—the width of three fingers, at arm's length), it also has a bright central disc, or "aureole," while the halo is just a ring of light. Nor should they confuse it with a glory (page 110), which appears in the opposite direction, looking away from the Sun.

Coronae can also be seen around car headlights viewed through a windscreen misted up with condensation. Anyone claiming cloud-collecting points for this is a terrible cheat.

Top: over the Channon Market, NSW, Australia, by Meggan Jack (Member 13764)

The width of a cloud's corona depends on the size of its droplets.

CLOUD-COLLECTING POINTS:

○ 20 points: Any corona

○ 15 points: Bonus for when the colors are distinct enough to extend from red through all the other colors to red again.

+ Add Total To Page 5

Seen in: thin Stratocumulus (p. 12), Stratus (p. 16), Altostratus (p. 20), Altocumulus (p. 18), Cirrostratus (p. 26), Cirrocumulus (p. 24).

Don't confuse with: glory (p. 110) or 22° halo (p. 120).

○ *I Spotted a corona*

DATE   TIME

LOCATION

WEATHER CONDITIONS

IMAGE FILE NAME(S)

Crepuscular Rays

Top: Rays fanning out from behind a Cumulus.
Bottom: Anti-crepuscular rays.

Even if they don't know the name, most cloudspotters will have plenty of opportunities to add crepuscular rays to their collection of cloud optical effects. They're the familiar sunbeams that appear to burst from behind a Cumulus cloud (page 10), or shine down through a hole in a Stratocumulus (page 12).

Crepuscular rays appear when the path of sunlight is made visible by tiny atmospheric particles too scarce to appear as cloud, but plentiful enough to scatter the light noticeably. Like fingers through a torch beam, the cloud shadows give edges to the rays. In spite of being almost parallel, these rays seem to radiate out from behind the cloud. This is just the same perspective effect as railway tracks seeming to widen as they get nearer.

Whenever you notice crepuscular rays from a low Sun, look to the opposite horizon for the far less obvious "anti-crepuscular rays." Appearing to emanate from a point directly opposite the Sun, these are the shadows cast by clouds behind you, like the shadow of someone shuffling behind you in a dusty cinema. Perspective makes them appear to converge in the distance. Few people ever notice anti-crepuscular rays—except vampire cloudspotters, eager for the arrival of night.

Top: over Gearr Aonach, Glencoe, Scotland, by John MacPherson (Member 10564)

"Jacob's ladder" occurs when crepuscular rays shine through holes in Stratocumulus.

CLOUD-COLLECTING POINTS:

○ 25 points: Any crepuscular rays

○ 20 points: Bonus for the much less obvious anti-crepuscular rays, which radiate from a point opposite the Sun

+ Add Total To Page 5

Seen in: (typically) Cumulus (p. 10) and Stratocumulus (p. 12), when water, dust and pollen particles scatter sunlight to show the cloud's shadow in 3-D.

○ *I spotted crepuscular rays*

DATE   TIME

LOCATION

WEATHER CONDITIONS

IMAGE FILE NAME(S)

Glory

Above: A glory seen through the fog from a bridge. ***Left:*** A glory around the shadow of a hang glider, flying over low cloud.

Cloudspotters must gain some elevation to add a glory to their collection of cloud optical effects, for this striking phenomenon is seen only with the Sun directly behind you, as it casts your shadow onto a layer of cloud. The glory, which looks like a series of rainbow rings around the shadow, is produced by cloud droplets reflecting, *refracting* and *diffracting* sunlight, although the exact optics are still not fully understood.

One of the easiest places to spot a glory is from that great cloudspotting location, the window of a plane. It can sometimes appear around the plane's shadow, cast on to a nearby layer of cloud or fog. When the cloud is some distance away, the shadow is absent, and you just see the colored rings.

Bonus cloud-collecting points are awarded for the most eerie form of glory—the "Brocken spectre." This is when the rings appear around your own shadow as you look at a cloud from a mountain ridge. The perspective can make the legs of your shadow flare out so, what with the multicolored halo, it looks like a ghost from the 1970s.

from the Golden Gate Bridge, San Francisco, US, by Mila Zinkova (Member 11067)

The Brocken spectre is a ghostly apparition caused by your own shadow.

CLOUD-COLLECTING POINTS:

○ 30 points: Any glory

○ 20 points: Bonus for all the effort of climbing a mountain and seeing a Brocken spectre (above)

+ Add Total To Page 5

Seen in: Stratus (p. 16), Altocumulus (p. 18), Altostratus (p. 20), fog (p. 90).

Don't confuse with: a corona (p. 106), which has similar colors but is a disc around the Sun, not your shadow.

○ *I spotted a glory*

DATE   TIME

LOCATION

WEATHER CONDITIONS

IMAGE FILE NAME(S)

Rainbow

When the sun is high, only the tip of the bow is visible.

We all love rainbows, but don't expect to earn many cloud-collecting points for seeing one. They're just too easy to notice. How ironic that rainbows, appearing on average about ten times a year (see note about the frequency of optical phenomena on page 144), are actually much less frequent than *halo phenomena* (see pages 120-131), which most people never notice.

To see a rainbow, look toward a rain shower with your back to the Sun, which must be no higher than 42 degrees above the horizon. (Unless you are looking down, from a high building, say.) Passing into each raindrop and reflecting off the back inner surface, the sunlight is *refracted* as it enters and leaves. The paths of its constituent wavelengths are bent by different amounts, separating out the colors. *Convection clouds* are the best sort for making rainbows, as they're more likely to produce showers when the sky around is clear, allowing direct sunlight to shine on them.

Besides the primary bow, a larger, fainter secondary bow can appear—the darker sky between the two being known as "Alexander's dark band." Within the primary bow, there are sometimes faint colored fringes, called "supernumerary bows."

Above: The best rainbows are produced by large raindrops, a few millimeters across.
Next Pages: Primary, secondary, and supernumerary bows, and Alexander's dark band.

CLOUD-COLLECTING POINTS:

○ 15 points: Any rainbow

○ 15 points: Bonus for a secondary bow, and for noticing Alexander's dark band between the two

+ Add Total To Page 5

Seen in: any rainfall in direct Sun— often from Cumulus congestus (p. 10) and Cumulonimbus (p. 30).

Don't confuse with: Circumzenithal arc (p. 128), halo phenomena (pp. 120-131).

○ *I spotted a rainbow*

DATE   TIME

LOCATION

WEATHER CONDITIONS

IMAGE FILE NAME(S)

secondary bow

Alexander's dark band

primary bow

primary bow

supernumerary bows

Cloudbow & Fogbow

Look for fogbows when the Sun shines brightly through thin fog or mist.

Cloudbows are like rainbows, but with much paler colors. In fact, they often don't show any discernible colors at all—looking like albino rainbows, or the ghosts of rainbows past. They appear as the sunlight is reflected and *refracted* by the tiny droplets that make up low- and midlevel clouds, rather than the much larger raindrops that produce rainbows (page 112).

In order to see a cloudbow, you have to be looking toward cloud droplets onto which the Sun is shining from directly behind your line of vision. Such a viewpoint is possible only from above clouds, which is why cloudbows are usually seen from a plane or a mountaintop. These are the same conditions in which to see the multicolored ring around your shadow, called a glory (page 110). If you see one, look for the other.

Cloudspotters wanting to add an albino rainbow to their collection, without taking to the air, should seek "fogbows." These are exactly the same, but appear in fog or mist (page 90).

Cloudbow and fogbow colors are pale or absent because, at less than 0.1 millimeter across, cloud droplets *diffract* sunlight more efficiently than larger raindrops, so the colors overlap more than those of a rainbow.

Over King Island, Bass Strait, Tasmania, Australia, by Nick Lovibond (Member 6851)

A cloudbow often appears at the same time as a glory (see bottom right of image).

CLOUD-COLLECTING POINTS:

O 35 points: Any cloudbow or fogbow

O 5 points: Bonus for managing to persuade someone that it actually is the ghost of a deceased rainbow

+ Add Total To Page 5

Seen in: Stratus (p. 16), Stratocumulus (p. 12), Altocumulus (p. 18), Altostratus (p. 20), fog/mist (p. 90).

Don't confuse with: rainbow (p. 112), glory (p. 110).

O *I spotted a cloudbow or fogbow*

DATE   TIME

LOCATION

WEATHER CONDITIONS

IMAGE FILE NAME(S)

22° Halo

The 22° halo is the most frequent of the many *halo phenomena* that can appear as sunlight is *refracted* through the ice crystals of thin layers of high clouds, such as Cirrus (page 22), Cirrostratus (page 26) and Cirrocumulus (page 24), or the ground-level ice-crystal cloud, diamond dust (page 94). Appearing on about 100 days of the year (see note about frequency on page 144), the 22° halo looks like a large ring around the Sun or Moon. Its inner edge generally has a reddish tinge to it, with the region of the sky between halo and Sun appearing darker than that just outside the halo. When cloud cover is less than extensive, only parts of the halo appear.

Cloudspotters observing a 22° halo for the first time will be surprised at how much larger it appears compared with photographs (wide-angle lenses are invariably used to make it fit the frame). The distance from Sun or Moon to the edge of the ring is equivalent to the outstretched span of a hand held up at arm's length.

Though it's worth 25 cloud-collecting points, a 22° halo is not worth screwing up your eyesight for, so take note of the halo-spotting safety advice on page 144.

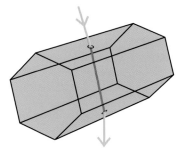

The **22° halo** can appear when a cloud's ice crystals have the shape of hexagonal columns. When these tumble in all directions, they refract the light most by an angle of 22°. Their combined sparkles form a ring of brighter light that appears as a halo around the Sun. To an observer, the angle between the Sun and the ring is 22°.

Above: The inner edge of a 22° halo often has a reddish tinge. *Next page:* Twinkles from countless ice crystals of Cirrostratus add up to make a 22° halo.

CLOUD-COLLECTING POINTS:

○ 25 points: Any 22° halo

○ 20 points: Bonus for a lunar 22° halo. This can appear around a full Moon but is usually too dim to show color

+ Add Total To Page 5

Seen in: Cirrostratus (p. 26), Cirrus (p. 22), Cirrocumulus (p. 24), diamond dust (p. 94).

Don't confuse with: the much smaller colored disc of a corona (p. 106).

○ *I Spotted a 22° halo*

DATE   TIME

LOCATION

WEATHER CONDITIONS

IMAGE FILE NAME(S)

Sundog

Also known as "mock suns" and "parhelia," sundogs are large spots of light that can appear on one or both sides of the Sun, and level with it. The second most frequent *halo phenomenon* after the 22° halo (page 120), sundogs appear on about 70 days of the year. (See note about frequency on page 144.) They are formed as sunlight is *refracted* through the ice crystals of thin layers of high clouds, such as Cirrus (page 22), Cirrostratus (page 26) and Cirrocumulus (page 24), or those of the ground-level ice-crystal cloud, diamond dust (page 94). The distance from the Sun of both spots of light is equivalent to the outstretched span of a hand held up at arm's length. Sundogs are brightest when the Sun is low, and visible only when it's below about 40 degrees from the horizon. If the cloud isn't in the right parts of the sky, just one sundog appears.

Cloudspotters should learn to recognize the sky that tends to produce sundogs, as well as the other halo phenomena. Scan the blue for light effects when it first pales with the subtle veil of ice-crystal clouds. (See page 144 for halo-spotting safety advice.) Once these are white enough to be noticed by the riffraff, they're generally too thick for sundogs.

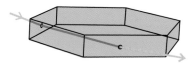

Sundogs can appear when a cloud's ice crystals are shaped like hexagonal plates and aligned almost horizontally (like falling leaves). When the Sun is very low in the sky, the crystals refract most light by 22 degrees, so observers see their collective sparkles as bright spots on either side of the Sun.

Above: A sundog has a reddish edge toward the Sun and a bluish-white tail away from it.
Next page: Sundogs always appear level with the Sun.

CLOUD-COLLECTING POINTS:

○ 20 points: One sundog

○ 15 points: Bonus for when sundogs appear on both sides of the Sun at the same time

+ Add Total To Page 5

Seen in: thin Cirrostratus (p. 26), Cirrus (p. 22), Cirrocumulus (p. 24), diamond dust (p. 94), contrails (p. 78).

Sun's elevation: below 40 degrees from horizon.

○ *I spotted a sundog*

DATE   TIME

LOCATION

WEATHER CONDITIONS

IMAGE FILE NAME(S)

Circumzenithal Arc

The ice crystals of Cirrus have found something to smile about.

The circumzenithal arc is a *halo phenomenon* that appears like a multicolored smile in the sky. Photographs of it look as if some fool's got a rainbow snap upside down, but this bow of colors actually appears in a totally different part of the sky from rainbows. On the 25 or so times a year that it appears (see note about frequency on page 144), it forms high up in the sky, like the fragment closest to the Sun of a circle around the zenith (directly up).

Whenever you notice the spots of light on either side of the Sun called sundogs (page 124), always look directly up (see page 144 for halo-spotting safety advice) because you might also be able to add this most beautiful of all halo phenomena to your collection of cloud optical effects, for it is produced by the same cloud ice crystals. It appears as sunlight is *refracted* by the ice crystals of thin layers of high clouds, such as Cirrus (page 22), Cirrostratus (page 26) and Cirrocumulus (page 24), or the ground-level ice-crystal cloud, diamond dust (page 94).

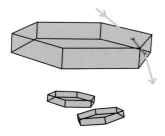

Circumzenithal arcs can appear when a cloud's ice crystals are in the shape of hexagonal plates and aligned more or less horizontally (like falling autumn leaves). As the light shines through the tops of the crystals and exits through a side face, the colors are separated and the combined sparkles appear as an arc.

A circumzenithal arc, high in the sky, formed by diamond dust.

CLOUD-COLLECTING POINTS:

○ 45 points: Any circumzenithal arc

○ 25 points: Bonus for when it appears at the same time as sundogs (p. 124)

+ Add Total To Page 5

Seen in: thin Cirrostratus (p. 26), Cirrus (p. 22), Cirrocumulus (p. 24), diamond dust (p. 94).

Sun's elevation: below 30 degrees from the horizon, but best when at 22 degrees.

○ *I spotted a circumzenithal arc*

DATE   TIME

LOCATION

WEATHER CONDITIONS

IMAGE FILE NAME(S)

Sun Pillars

Like many halo phenomena, pillars can also be seen by the light of a full Moon.

Sun pillars are vertical streaks of light that appear above and below a low Sun as it shines through ice-crystal clouds, such as Cirrus (page 22), Cirrostratus (page 26) and Cirrocumulus (page 24), or the ground-level ice-crystal cloud, diamond dust (page 94). At night, they are called "moon pillars."

These *halo phenomena*, which appear on about 25 days of the year (see note about frequency on page 144), are due to sunlight reflecting off the surface of ice crystals. They are akin to "glitter paths" that shine on the rippled surface of the sea. The pillar extending above the Sun appears brightest when the Sun is just below the horizon.

Most halo phenomena look best when the clouds' crystals are optically pure, regularly shaped and neatly aligned, but this is not the case for sun pillars. The light needs only to glance off a surface, so the crystals can be rough, irregular and jumbled. The poor man's halo phenomena, they often appear when cloud crystals aren't quite right for the more refined arcs, rings and spots of light to form (see pages 120-131).

Forms upper pillar

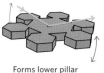

Forms lower pillar

Crystals wobble or spin

Sun pillars form when the sunlight reflects off the surface of the cloud's ice crystals. These need to be wobbling or rotating about a horizontal axis as they fall through the air for tall pillars to appear.

The best sun pillars appear just after the Sun has dipped below the horizon.

CLOUD-COLLECTING POINTS:

○ 35 points: Any sun/moon pillars

○ 10 points: Bonus for a pillar below the Sun, seen from a plane, which contains a bright patch, called a subsun

+ Add Total To Page 5

Seen in: Cirrostratus (p. 26), Cirrus (p. 22), Cirrocumulus (p. 24), diamond dust (p. 94).

Sun's elevation: visible when Sun is less than 5 degrees above horizon; clearest when Sun is 2 degrees below horizon.

○ *I spotted a sun pillar or moon pillar*

DATE   TIME

LOCATION

WEATHER CONDITIONS

IMAGE FILE NAME(S)

Technical Terms

It's hard to explain clouds without sometimes using technical language. When the cloud entries have required this, the term has been written in italics and an explanation with respect to clouds is given below. Where explanations refer to other technical terms, these appear here in italics too.

Accessory clouds: Those that form close to one of the main cloud types, with which they sometimes merge. (See pp. 50-55.)

Cloudlets: An extended layer of cloud can be either smooth and continuous or made up of discernible clumps of cloud. These clumps, which can be joined or separate, are cloudlets.

Cloud levels: For the purpose of classifying clouds, meteorologists divide the *troposphere* into three arbitrary levels, or "étages": low, medium and high. Clouds associated with each level are those whose bases are typically found within its altitude range.

Condensation nuclei: The plentiful tiny particles, floating in the atmosphere, that are the right size and shape to act as "seeds" on which *water vapor* can start to condense to form cloud droplets. Just a few thousandths of a millimeter in size, they might be particles of salt (from the sea), dust (minerals, dead vegetation), ash or man-made pollution.

Convection clouds: Those that are formed by rising *convection currents* of air. By expanding as they rise, the currents can cool enough for some of their *water vapor* to condense into cloud droplets. (See pp. 10 and 30.)

Convection currents: Air rising (or sinking) as a result of being heated (or cooled) and therefore becoming less dense (or denser) than the surrounding air. An example is a thermal, when air, warmed by the Sun-baked ground, floats upward.

Diffraction: How light waves spread out as they pass around tiny obstacles, such as cloud droplets or ice crystals. Different wavelengths are spread by different degrees and, if the cloud particles are of uniform size, each wavelength can produce an interference pattern of bright and dark fringes. The result is bands of different colored light. (See pp. 102, 106, 110, 112, 118.)

Genera of cloud: The ten main classifications of cloud (see pp. 10-31). Clouds can belong to just one genus at a time.

Halo phenomena: Optical effects that result from the reflection and *refraction* of light as it passes through ice-crystal clouds. When optically pure and regularly shaped, the crystals can act as tiny prisms that bend or disperse the light. Those at certain angles from the Sun are more likely than others to shine light at an observer. Their combined sparkles are what produce white or colored arcs, rings and spots of light across the sky. (See pp. 120-131.)

Icing nuclei: Particular airborne particles that can act as the "seeds" onto which liquid cloud droplets can start to freeze into ice crystals. While there are generally plenty of *condensation nuclei* around, icing ones can be quite scarce. Without them, droplets can remain *supercooled* until temperatures drop to around -40 degrees F. A lack of suitable icing nuclei is why clouds often remain in the form of supercooled droplets below 32 degrees F.

Mesosphere: The region of the atmosphere that is above the *stratosphere*, with an altitude range from 30 to more than 50 miles. It's the coldest part of the atmosphere, where temperatures drop to -195 degrees F, and home to the Earth's highest clouds (see p. 98).

Multicell storm: A thunderstorm, in which more than one "cell" is active at once. Each cell is a system of rising and falling air currents, which combine to form a large Cumulonimbus (p. 30) cloud structure. As air rushes in at the base to feed the vertical growth of one cell, it can trigger another cell to start building at the front of the storm, which appears as a rising cloud tower. Though less coordinated than in a *supercell storm*, this succession of cells can extend the storm's duration for many hours.

Refraction: The way light changes direction as it passes between air and the water droplets or ice crystals of a cloud. Since different wavelengths are bent by different degrees, this generally leads to the sunlight being separated into its constituent colors. (See pp. 112, 120-129.)

Species of cloud: Cloud classification, by which some of the ten main cloud types, or *genera*, are subdivided. A cloud of a particular genus can belong to just one species at a time. For a table of all the formal cloud classifications, see p. 136.

Stable air: A region of the atmosphere in which a parcel of air tends to sink back down or rise back up to its original level when displaced, due to the way temperature varies with altitude.

Stratosphere: The region of the atmosphere above the *troposphere* and below the *mesosphere*, with an altitude range of 12 to 30 miles. It is separated from the turbulent air currents nearer the ground by a *temperature inversion*, called the *tropopause*. The only clouds that enter the stratosphere are nacreous (p. 96) and the tops of huge Cumulonimbus (p. 30).

Supercell storm: A very large, violent and persistent thunderstorm, consisting of a self-organizing structure of Cumulonimbus cloud (p. 30). The storm's up- and downdrafts become coordinated to feed and maintain the cloud's structure, often for several hours and over long distances. Supercell storms can produce strong winds, frequent lightning, torrential rain, large hailstones and tornadoes.

Supercooled droplets: Cloud droplets that refuse to freeze, even though they are below 32 degrees F. Midlevel clouds, such as Altocumulus (p. 18), are often supercooled. Unless there are enough *icing nuclei* to facilitate freezing, water can remain in droplet form at temperatures as low as -40 degrees F.

Supplementary features: Cloud forms that only appear attached to one of the main types of cloud, or *genera*. (See pp. 56-71.)

Temperature inversion: Normally, the air gets colder as you rise through the *troposphere*. An inversion is when, within a certain altitude range, this fall-off in temperature is arrested, or temperatures actually increase with height. Such a temperature profile acts as a "thermal ceiling" that tends to halt the vertical growth of clouds. Inversions can occur at any altitude in the troposphere, the top of which is defined in terms of an inversion, called the *tropopause*. This is what causes large Cumulonimbus clouds to splay out in an anvil shape (see pp. 30, 70).

Tropopause: The *temperature inversion* that marks the boundary between the *troposphere* and the *stratosphere*.

Troposphere: The lower region of the atmosphere, up to about eight miles in the midlatitudes, higher at the tropics and lower at the poles. This is the turbulent region where Earth's weather is generated. Almost all clouds form within the troposphere, the two exceptions being nacreous (p. 96) and noctilucent (p. 98).

Unstable air: A region of the atmosphere in which a parcel of air displaced up- or downward has a tendency to keep going, due to the way the temperature varies with altitude.

Varieties of cloud: A visual characteristic that's used in the classification of clouds. Any cloud can exhibit several of these at once, and so belong to more than one variety at a time. For a table of all the official cloud classifications, see p. 136.

Water vapor: The gaseous state of water. Clouds appear when this invisible gas, one of the most variable components of air, forms into liquid droplets or solid ice crystals, which are visible.

Cloud Classification

Clouds are officially classified according to a Latin Linnean system (like the one used for plants and animals), based on their height and appearance. While the system isn't comprehensive, most clouds fall into one of the ten basic *genera*. They can further be defined as one of the possible *species*, and any of the possible *varieties*. *Accessory clouds* and *supplementary features* are ones often found near particular genera. Genera are spelled with a capital letter. The numbers in parentheses refer to the relevant pages.

Level	Genus	Species (can only be one)	Varieties (can be more than one)	Accessory Clouds & Supp. Features
Low Clouds	Cumulus (10)	humilis mediocris congestus fractus	radiatus (46)	pileus (50) velum (52) virga (60) praecipitatio arcus (64) pannus (54) tuba (68)
	Stratocumulus (12)	stratiformis lenticularis (34) castellanus (40)	translucidus perlucidus opacus duplicatus (48) undulatus (42) radiatus (46) lacunosus (44)	mamma (56) virga (60) praecipitatio
	Stratus (16)	nebulosus fractus	opacus translucidus undulatus (42)	praecipitatio

Level	Genus	Species (can only be one)	Varieties (can be more than one)	Accessory Clouds & Supp. Features
Midlevel Clouds	Altocumulus (18)	stratiformis lenticularis (34) castellanus (40) floccus	translucidus perlucidus opacus duplicatus (48) undulatus (42) radiatus (46) lacunosus (44)	virga (60) mamma (56)
	Altostratus (20)	(none)	translucidus opacus duplicatus (48) undulatus (42) radiatus (46)	virga (60) praecipitatio pannus (54) mamma (56)
High Clouds	Cirrus (22)	fibratus (38) uncinus spissatus castellanus (40) floccus	intortus radiatus (46) vertebratus duplicatus (48)	mamma (56)
	Cirrocumulus (24)	stratiformis lenticularis (34) castellanus (40) floccus	undulatus (42) lacunosus (44)	virga (60) mamma (56)
	Cirrostratus (26)	fibratus (38) nebulosus	duplicatus (48) undulatus (42)	(none)
Multilevel Clouds	Nimbostratus (28) (extends through more than one level)	(none)	(none)	praecipitatio virga (60) pannus (54)
	Cumulonimbus (30) (extends through all three levels)	calvus capillatus	(none)	praecipitatio virga (60) pannus (54) incus (70) mamma (56) pileus (50) velum (52) arcus (64) tuba (68)

Photographers Index

We are very grateful to all the members of the Cloud Appreciation Society who agreed to contribute clouds from their collections to illustrate this handbook. All image copyrights remain with the photographers.

Cloud Image Index

When parts of the sky bear similarities to these thumbnails, refer to the page numbers to see what the cloud types might be.

10

22

30, 70

12

24

34

16, 90

26

38, 26

18

26, 22, 24, 94

40, 18

20

28, 20

18, 42

22

30, 70

42, 12

44, 18

64, 30

82, 64

46, 22

68, 30

84

18

72, 34

84, 78

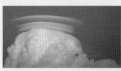

50, 10, 30

72, 18

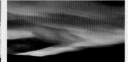

88

54, 28, 30

76

96

56, 30

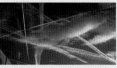

78

98

60, 18

80

A photograph may illustrate
more than one type of cloud—
hence multiple page numbers.
For optical effects caused by
clouds, see pp. 102–131.

Index

The main entries for clouds are in **bold**.

Final Notes

You can become a member of the Cloud Appreciation Society by visting www.cloudappreciationsociety.org. The Web site has advice about photographing clouds and a gallery where you can post your prized cloud images.

Anyone who wants to know more about cloud optical phenomena should visit the Atmospheric Optics Web site run by Les Cowley (member 14) at www.atoptics.co.uk.

If you're interested in finding out about the weather in general, you might consider joining the Royal Meteorological Society. It publishes a monthly journal, *Weather*, and holds meetings every year for those interested in weather and climate. You can find out more at www.rmets.org.

The cloud charts on the endpapers were illustrated by Anthony Haythornthwaite (member 2367), who can be contacted at anthony@aqhthestudio.co.uk.

A cautionary note about observing halo phenomena:
Ice-crystal clouds that give rise to halo phenomena (see pages 120-131) block very little of the Sun's rays. Always shield both eyes from the Sun when looking at them. It's a good idea to stand so that a building, a tree or a nearby giraffe shields the Sun itself from your vision. Special care should be taken when photographing halo phenomena with an SLR camera, as the viewfinder will tend to increase the chance of retinal damage from direct rays.

Frequency of optical phenomena:
All figures of the frequency of occurrence of haloes and other optical phenomena are based on observations made over Germany, between 1986 and 2004, that were compiled by the German "Meteor Work Group": www.meteoros.de.

45,000 ft
CIRRUS
40,000 ft
35,000 ft
30,000 ft
CIRROSTRATUS
25,000 ft
20,000 ft
ALTOSTRATUS
15,000 ft
10,000 ft
NIMBOSTRATUS
STRATOCUMULUS
5,000 ft
STRATUS
0 ft